T0058518

by Michael P. Wolfsohn

HAL•LEONARD™
CORPORATION

7777 W. BLUEMOUND RD. P.O. BOX 13819 MILWAUKEE, WI 53213

About This Book

*T*his book has been designed to be more than just a catalog of chords. It is intended as a multi-function harmonic reference source for guitarists.

The key to its usefulness is in its organization — it is organized around each chord's root note and harmonic function rather than around root notes alone. This allows it to work in three ways:

- **as a chord dictionary**

- **as a chord substitution guide**

- **as a harmonic reference**

This book will be a powerful tool and an important aid to your musical development.

How To Use This Book

*Y*ou may use this book in three different ways:

- **As a chord dictionary**:

  when you encounter an unfamiliar chord in music that you wish to play, you may look it up here, just as you would look up an unfamiliar word in an English language dictionary.

- **As a chord substitution guide**:

  when you are trying to decide what kind of chord to put into a progression, or are looking for a better sounding chord to substitute for one that you find in sheet music, you may look it up here. In addition, there is a reference section that explains how chord substitutions work, and which chords may be substituted for which other chords.

- **As a harmonic guide:**

  when you are looking for the next chord that would commonly occur in a chord progression (whether you wish to to use it or to avoid it) you may look it up here. There are also a number of sections that explain chord progressions and other important considerations in music theory.

Guide to Notation

*T*wo different kinds of notation are used in this book —
guitar tablature (with standard notation) and chord frames.
They are used for different purposes and will be explained
on this page and the following page.

Tablature

*G*uitar tablature (TAB) is a special staff that graphically
represents the guitar fingerboard. Each line represents
one string on the guitar. The numbers on these lines
indicate at which frets to place your fingers. The number
"0" indicates an open (unfingered) string.
Here are some examples of tablature:

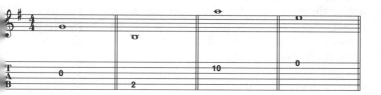

Tablature alone does not provide any rhythmic information.
For that and other reasons, it is usually coupled with standard
notation. Here are the same examples of tablature, this time
coupled with standard notation:

Tablature coupled with standard notation will be used
throughout this book.

Chord Frames

*A*nother way that guitar music can be graphically represented is through the use of chord frames. A chord frame consists of a grid that represents a portion of the guitar neck. Vertical lines represent strings and horizontal lines represent frets. Dots placed on the vertical lines represent the locations at which fingers should be placed.

While all chord frames use at least the elements listed above, there are many different ways that additional information can be incorporated into the basic chord frame. Here are some examples of the type of chord frames that are used in this book:

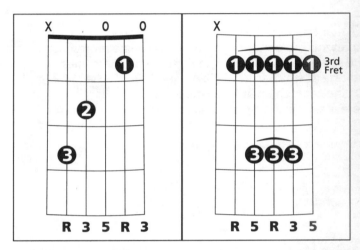

First, let's talk about what is common to these two chord frames. Each grid represents a playing area of four consecutive frets. The six vertical lines represent (from left to right) strings 6 (Low E) through 1 (High E). The numbers in the circles on the string lines represent the left hand fingers — 1 is the index finger, 2 is the middle finger, 3 is the ring finger and 4 is the little finger. The numbers below the grid represent chord degrees (more about this later on in the book). The letter **"R"** below the grid represents the root (or name tone) of the chord. Since both of these are C major chords, the root for each of them is the note "C". An **X** above the grid indicates a string which is **not** part of the chord, and is **not** to be played — the string will have to be either muted or avoided. A **0** above the grid indicates an open (unfingered) string.

Now, let's examine the differences.

The chord frame on the left represents a chord in first position Frets 1-4). The heavy line at the top of the grid represents the nut of the guitar; the thin line below it represents the first fret, etc.

The chord frame on the right represents a chord in third position (Frets 3-7). The indicator **"3rd fret"** to the right of the grid indicates the position.. The thin line at the top, then,represents the **second** fret, the **next** thin line below that represents the **third** fret. A curved line above a group of dots with the same finger number in them represents a **barre**. Dots and numbers below the grid in grey represent optional notes — notes that may be played but are not required to form the chord.

Half steps and Whole steps

*T*he chords in this book are grouped by **harmonic function** — the role they play in standard chord progressions. In order to get the most use out of this book, an understanding of harmonic functions is important.

Understanding harmonic functions will require some understanding of music theory. While some music theory topics will be covered in this book, you can gain a more thorough understanding of theory by consulting one of the many excellent books and courses now available that deal with music theory exclusively and in depth, such as *Music Theory for Guitar* from the Guitar Techniques series available from Hal Leonard.

Meanwhile this book will explain basic music theory from half steps and whole steps through harmonic functions.

The basic building block of music is the half step. A half step is the distance between any given note and the nearest next possible note. On the guitar, this is a distance of one fret.

A whole step is the same distance as two consecutive half steps, or (on the guitar) a distance of two frets.

Here are some example of half steps and whole steps:

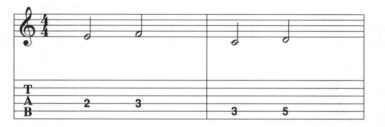

half step   whole step

Notice that the distance between the notes stays the same (and sounds the same) no matter where on the guitar the notes are played. The distance between C and D, for example, is always a whole step whether they are both on the same string, or not:

whole step   whole step

Major Scales

*O*nce you understand half steps and whole steps, you are ready to learn about major scales. A major scale is a sequence of eight notes that meets the following criteria:

1. It proceeds through all the notes in letter name order, with none skipped or repeated.
   This also means that on a standard notation staff, a major scale proceeds through consecutive lines and spaces with none skipped or repeated.

2. The first note and the last note have the same letter name. The last note is an octave higher than the first.

3. It may contain sharps or flats, but not both.

4. It proceeds through the following sequence of half steps and whole steps:

   whole – whole – half – whole – whole – whole – half

Every major scale meets these requirements. Here, for example is a C major scale with the half steps and whole steps shown:

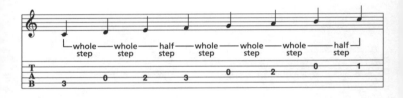

Sharps and flats are added to make the scale conform to the required sequence of half steps and whole steps. Here is a table showing which sharps and flats must be added to make major scales on any of the twelve notes:

Key	Sharps/Flats
C#	F#,C#,G#,D#,A#, E#, B#
D	F#,C#
E♭	B♭, E♭, A♭
E	F#,C#,G#, D#
F	B♭
F#	F#,C#,G#,D#,A#, E#
G	F#
A♭	B♭, E♭, A♭, D♭
A	F#,C#,G#
B♭	B♭, E♭
B	F#,C#,G#,D#,A#

Intervals

*T*he next step toward understanding harmonic functions is to understand intervals. An interval is the distance between two notes, as measured on the staff.

Each interval has two names, a general name (second third, etc.) which refers to the number of note names the two notes are apart from each other, and a specific name, (Major, Minor, etc.) which refers to the color of the interval. Intervals belong to one of two families, the Major/Minor family or the Perfect family.

Here is a table of intervals:

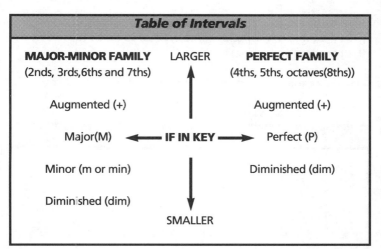

Table of Intervals

MAJOR-MINOR FAMILY (2nds, 3rds,6ths and 7ths)	LARGER	PERFECT FAMILY (4ths, 5ths, octaves(8ths))
Augmented (+)		Augmented (+)
Major(M)	IF IN KEY	Perfect (P)
Minor (m or min)		Diminished (dim)
Diminished (dim)	SMALLER	

To identify an interval, first find its general name, by counting the number of letter names between the two notes, including the names of both notes. You get the same result by counting the number of lines and spaces between the two notes on the standard notation staff, including the lines or spaces on which both notes are sitting.

Then find the specific name by doing the following:

1. Find the major scale that begins on the lower of the two notes. If the upper note is in that scale, then the interval is major (if it belongs to the Major/Minor family) or perfect (if it belongs to the Perfect family).

2. If the upper note is not in the scale, determine how many half steps closer together or farther apart the two notes are than they would be if the upper note was in the scale. Then move up or down the chart that number of half steps to find the specific name of the interval.

Here are a few examples of intervals with their names shown:

1	Minor seventh
2	Augmented fifth
3	Augmented second
4	Diminished fifth

Triads and Sevenths

*T*riads and sevenths are the two types of chords used in describing harmonic functions.

A triad is a three note chord with the notes in specific intervallic relationships. The lowest of the three notes is called the **root** (or name tone). The interval from the root to the middle note will always be some type of third, and the interval from the root to the upper note will always be some type of fifth.

Notice that all the intervals are intervals from the root. This is also true when you build larger chords, such as sevenths.

A seventh is a four note chord that contains a third and a fifth (just like a triad) plus some type of seventh (between the root and the highest note).

Here is a table of triads, followed by a table of sevenths:

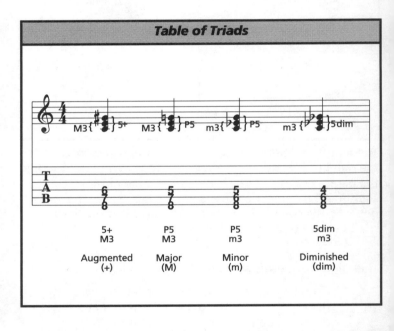

5+	P5	P5	5dim
M3	M3	m3	m3
Augmented (+)	Major (M)	Minor (m)	Diminished (dim)

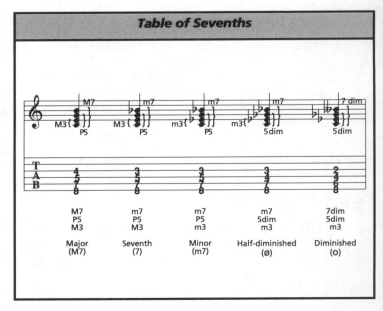

M7	m7	m7	m7	7dim
P5	P5	P5	5dim	5dim
M3	M3	m3	m3	m3
Major (M7)	Seventh (7)	Minor (m7)	Half-diminished (ø)	Diminished (o)

Diatonic Triads

The triads built on the steps of a major scale are called diatonic triads. These are all of the triads possible in a major key. Any other triad will be out of key.

To construct diatonic triads, begin by writing out a major scale. Then build triads on each note of the scale, using only the notes in that scale, and no others.

Starting on C, you would get these triads:

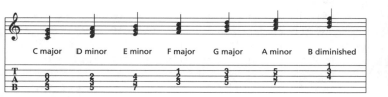

This sequence of triads (major, minor, minor, major, major, minor, diminished) is referred to as the **diatonic triads** for a given major key, and, like the pattern of half steps and whole steps holds true for **any** major key.

Diatonic triads are commonly referred to by the scale degree of their roots. In Roman numerals this would be as follows:

I — ii — iii — IV — V — vi — vii(dim) — I

Numerals in upper case refer to major chords, numerals in lower case refer to minor chords. The single oddity is the diminished chord built on the seventh degree of the scale. It is rarely used, and you will probably not encounter it.

Diatonic seventh chords may be constructed in the same way. The only one that concerns us right now is the one built on the fifth (or dominant) degree of the scale. This seventh chord, which consists of a major third, a perfect fifth and a minor third, is called a dominant-type seventh. It is customary to refer to these chords simply as "sevenths".

Here are the diatonic triads for C major with a seventh chord on V

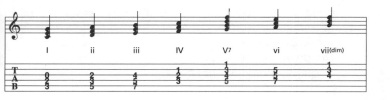

Harmonic Functions

*T*here are only three roles that a chord can play within a major key. It can function as a **major** chord, a **minor** chord or a **dominant seventh** chord.

Let's look at what each of these chords does within a major key.

Major chords serve as anchors in the key.

They help to define it as a major key. The most important major chord in a major key is, of course the one built on the name tone for that key. Thus, in the key of C major, the C major chord is the **tonic** or **I** chord. Music in major keys tends to end on the **I** chord In fact, a piece of music in the key of C could be thought of as being basically a series of chords designed to lead around to a final C chord at the end. Major chords can also be found on the fourth and fifth degrees of the scale. These are considered the pillar chords of the key. Every note in the scale can be harmonized by one of these major chords.

Minor chords add color to the key.

While every note in a major key can be harmonized by one of the three major chords in the key, music written with nothing but major chords can become dull. Minor chords help relieve this dullness by adding a different color (or sound quality) to music. Minor chords also help chord progressions along by their tendency to move to the chord (within the key) that is built on the note four scale steps above their own roots. For example, in the key of C, D minor tends to move to G7, E minor tends to move to A minor, and A minor tends to move to D minor.

Dominant seventh chords define the key.

Of the three types of chords, dominant sevenths are unique in several ways. First, while there are two majors and three minors in any key, the dominant seventh can only be built in one place — on the fifth (or dominant) degree of the scale. Second, while both major and minor chords are **consonant** (they can stand on their own), the dominant seventh is **dissonant** (it must resolve to another chord, in this case the tonic or **I** chord). The need for the dominant (or **V7**) chord to resolve to the tonic is so strong that this progression alone defines a key. That is, when you hear a G7 chord resolve to a C major chord, you know immediately that you are in the key of C major. The seventh chord built on the fifth degree of the major scale (V7) is called the **dominant** because it *dominates* the key: it single-handedly *defines* the key.

Chord Substitution and Alterations

Since there are only three harmonic functions, all other chords can be thought of as substitutes for or chromatic alterations of one of the three.

Substitute chords are usually employed to disguise or "soften" the effect of a major, minor or (especially) seventh chord. For example, the ninth chord (which is a seventh chord with a major ninth interval added to make a five note chord) functions identically to a seventh chord, but is not as harsh in sound.

Here are two **V-I** progressions in C major:

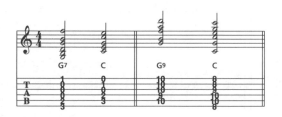

Notice that while both the G7 and G9 chords are dissonant and want to resolve to C major, the ninth chord in the second progression is less dissonant, or softer, and has less of a need to resolve.

Similarly, other chords can be substituted for any of the three function chords to change the effect without changing the function.

Chords can also be chromatically altered. The most common alterations are the raising or lowering (sharping or flatting) of the fifth or ninth degree in chords that function as either minors or sevenths.
This is usually done for one of two reasons:

1. If a note in the melody of a song is one of these notes, the chord is frequently altered to match the melody.

2. A chord may be altered to create a particular melodic or bass line motion. For example the chord progression C-Am-Dm-G may be altered as follows in order to create a melody that descends by half steps:

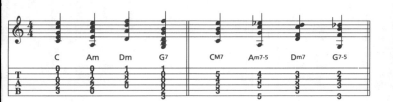

*J*ust as triads are constructed of three notes in specific intervallic relationships, so other chords are constructed of specified intervals. On these two pages you will find tables showing the intervallic construction of 36 commonly used chords. (Tables for triads and seventh chords are on page 8.)

While tablature is given for all of these chords to show you where the notes are on the guitar, not all of these particular root position chord forms can actually be played on the guitar. None of the seven note chords, for example, can be played as written because the guitar has only six strings. Some of the five and six note chords would require five or six left-hand fingers to play as written.

The tablature on these two pages, then, is for reference

Chord Construction

Five Note Chords

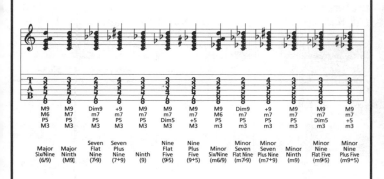

M9	M9	Dim9	+9	M9	M9	M9	M9	M9	Dim9	+9	M9	M9	M9
M6	M7	m7	m7	m7	m7	m7	M6	M7	m7	m7	m7	m7	m7
P5	P5	P5	P5	P5	P5	Dim5	P5	P5	P5	P5	P5	Dim5	+5
M3	M3	M3	M3	M3	M3	M3	M3	m3	m3	m3	m3	m3	m3

| Major Six/Nine (6/9) | Major Ninth (M9) | Seven Flat Nine (7♭9) | Seven Plus Nine (7+9) | Ninth (9) | Nine Flat Five (9♭5) | Nine Plus Five (9+5) | Minor Six/Nine (m6/9) | Minor Seven Flat Nine (m7♭9) | Minor Seven Plus Nine (m7+9) | Minor Ninth (m9) | Minor Nine Flat Five (m9♭5) | Minor Nine Plus Five (m9+5) |

Six Note Chords

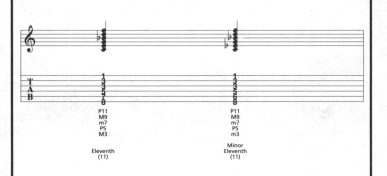

P11	P11
M9	M9
m7	m7
P5	P5
M3	m3

| Eleventh (11) | Minor Eleventh (11) |

Seven Note Chords

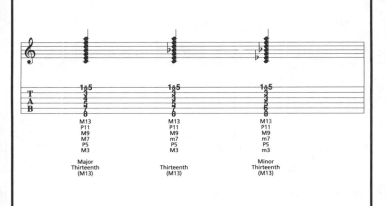

M13	M13	M13
P11	P11	P11
M9	M9	M9
M7	m7	m7
P5	P5	P5
M3	M3	m3

| Major Thirteenth (M13) | Thirteenth (M13) | Minor Thirteenth (M13) |

Necessary Notes in Chords

*N*ot every note in a chord is necessary for its color and harmonic function to be heard clearly. This table tells you which notes are in a chord, which are required, which are preferred although not required, and which are not needed. (All flats and sharps are as compared to a major scale.)

Major Chords

Chord	All Notes	Required	Preferred	Other
M	R,3,5	R,3,5		
sus4	R,4,5	R,4,5		
M6	R,3,5,6	R,3,6	5	
Madd9	R,3,5,9	R,3,9	5	
M7	R,3,5,7	R,3,7	5	
M6/9	R,3,5,6,9	R,3,6,9	5	
M9	R,3,5,7,9	R,3,7,9	5	
M13	R,3,5,7,9,13	R,3,7,13	5	9

Minor Chords

Chord	All Notes	Required	Preferred	Other
m	R,♭3,5	R,♭3,5		
m6	R,♭3,5,6	R,♭3,6	5	
m7	R,♭3,5,♭7	R,♭3,♭7	5	
m7-5	R,♭3,♭5,♭7	R,♭3,♭5,♭7		
m7+5	R,♭3,+5,♭7	R,♭3,+5,♭7		
mM7	R,♭3,5,7	R,♭3,7	5	
m6/9	R,♭3,5,6,9	R,♭3,6,9	5	
m7-9	R,♭3,5,♭7,♭9	R,♭3,♭7,♭9	5	
m7+9	R,♭3,5,♭7,+9	R,♭3,♭7,+9	5	
m9	R,♭3,5,♭7,9	R,♭3,♭7,9	5	

Minor Chords (cont)				
Chord	**All Notes**	**Required**	**Preferred**	**Other**
m9-5	R,b3,b5,b7,9	R,b3,b5,b7,9		
m9+5	R,b3,+5,b7,9	R,b3,+5,b7,9		
m11	R,b3,5,b7,9,11	R,b3,b7,11	5	9
m13	R,b3,5,b7,9,11,13	R,b3,b7,9,13	5	9,11

Seventh Chords				
Chord	**All Notes**	**Required**	**Preferred**	**Other**
dim	R,b3,b5	R,b3,b5		
+	R,3,+5	R,3,+5		
7	R,3,5,b7	R,3,b7	5	
7sus4	R,4,5,b7	R,4,b7	5	
7-5	R,3,b5,b7	R,3,b5,b7		
7+5	R,3,+5,b7	R,3,+5,b7		
dim7	R,b3,b5,dim7	R,b3,b5,dim7		
7-9	R,3,5,b7,b9	R,3,b7,b9	5	
7+9	R,3,5,b7,+9	R,3,b7,+9	5	
9	R,3,5,b7,9	R,3,b7,9	5	
9-5	R,3,b5,b7,9	R,3,b5,b7,9		
9+5	R,3,+5,b7,9	R,3,+5,b7,9		
11	R,3,5,b7,9,11	R,3,5,b7,9,11	5	9
13	R,3,5,b7,9,11,13	R,3,b7,13	5	9,11

Table of Chord Substitutions

*T*his table tells you which of the three harmonic functions these 36 chords serve. It will also tell you which of the 33 altered chords are always, usually or seldom acceptable substitutes for the 3 original, unaltered harmonic function chords.

Function	Always	Usually	Seldom
Major	Major Sixth	Major Seventh	Major Ninth
	Major Six / Nine	Major Thirteenth	
	Major add 9	Suspended Fourth	
Minor	Minor Seventh	Minor Sixth	Minor Seven $\flat$5
	Minor Ninth	Minor Six / Nine	Minor Seven $\flat$5 / Minor Seven +5
		Minor Eleventh	Minor Seven $\flat$9 / Minor Seven +5
		Minor Thirteenth	Minor Nine $\flat$5 / Minor Nine +5
Seventh	Seventh Suspended Fourth	Seven $\flat$5	
	Ninth	Seven +5	
	Eleventh	Seven $\flat$9*	
	Thirteenth	Seven +9	
	Augmented	Nine $\flat$5	
	Diminished*	Nine +5	
	Diminished Seventh*		

* The diminished and diminished seventh chords must be built on the note one half step above the root of the seventh chord that they are replacing. They function as a seven $\flat$9 chord with no root and with the $\flat$9 in the bass

Table of Major Triads
(Strings 1-4)

*T*he table on this page gives you three movable forms for major triads on strings 1 through 4, and tells you which triad you are playing at each position from open to 12th fret. Above the 12th fret, the table repeats — simply subtract 12 from the fret number to find the triad on this table.

All of these triads are in **close position**: each successively higher note is the next possible chord tone.

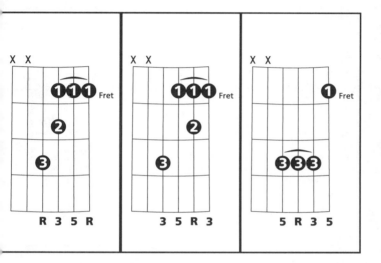

Root Position		First Inversion*		Second Inversion*	
Fret	Chord	Fret	Chord	Fret	Chord
0	E	0	C	0	A
1	F	1	C#/Db	1	A#/Bb
2	F#/Gb	2	D	2	B
3	G	3	D#/Eb	3	C
4	G#/Ab	4	E	4	C#/Db
5	A	5	F	5	D
6	A#/Bb	6	F#/Gb	6	D#/Eb
7	B	7	G	7	E
8	C	8	G#/Ab	8	F
9	C#/Db	9	A	9	F#/Gb
10	D	10	A#/Bb	10	G
11	D#/Eb	11	B	11	G#/Ab
12	E	12	C	12	A

* An inversion of a chord refers to the same notes in a different sequence. Here, root position has the root of the chord as its lowest tone; first inversion has the 3rd of the chord as the lowest note; and second inversion has the 5th of the chord as the lowest note.

Table of Minor Triads
(Strings 1-4)

*T*his table gives you three movable forms for minor triads on strings 1 through 4.

These triads are in also in close position (they are the same triads from the Major triads table on page 17, with the third degree of each triad lowered one half step to form the minor). Again, you may play strings 1, 2, & 3, strings 2, 3, & 4 or strings 1 through 4 and still play the complete triad.

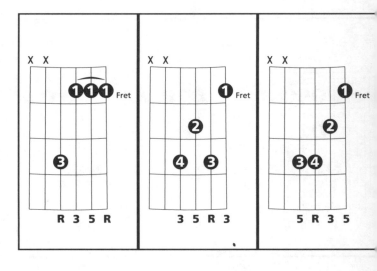

Root Position		First Inversion*		Second Inversion*	
Fret	Chord	Fret	Chord	Fret	Chord
0	Em	0	C#m/D♭m	0	Am
1	Fm	1	Dm	1	A#m/B♭m
2	F#m/G♭m	2	D#m/E♭m	2	Bm
3	G	3	Em	3	Cm
4	G#m/A♭m	4	Fm	4	C#m/D♭m
5	Am	5	F#m/G♭m	5	Dm
6	A#m/B♭m	6	Gm	6	D#m/E♭m
7	Bm	7	G#m/A♭m	7	Em
8	Cm	8	Am	8	Fm
9	C#m/D♭m	9	A#m/B♭m	9	F#m/G♭m
10	Dm	10	Bm	10	Gm
11	D#m/E♭m	11	Cm	11	G#m/A♭m
12	Em	12	C#m/D♭m	12	Am

* An inversion of a chord refers to the same notes in a different sequence. Here, root position has the root of the chord as its lowest tone; first inversion has the 3rd of the chord as the lowest note; and second inversion has the 5th of the chord as the lowest note.

Table of Sevenths
(Strings 1-4)

Small seventh chords work a little differently on the guitar than triads do.

Since there are four notes in a seventh chord, there are four possible inversions. Also, because there are four notes, you must play all four strings to play the complete seventh chord.

Close position sevenths are very awkward on the guitar, and therefore are not very useful. The forms given in this table are the ones that are most commonly used.

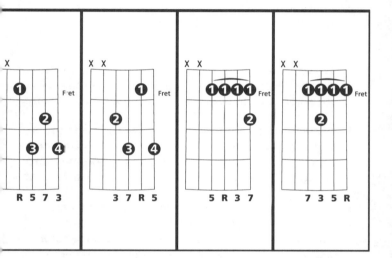

Root Position		First Inversion*		Second Inversion*		Third Inversion*	
Fret	Chord	Fret	Chord	Fret	Chord	Fret	Chord
0	D7	0	B7	0	G7	0	E7
1	D#7/Eb7	1	C7	1	G#7/Ab7	1	F7
2	E7	2	C#7/Db7	2	A7	2	F#7/Gb7
3	F7	3	D7	3	A#7/Bb7	3	G7
4	F#7/Gb7	4	D#7/Eb7	4	B7	4	G#7/Ab7
5	G7	5	E7	5	C7	5	A7
6	G#7/Ab7	6	F7	6	C#7/Db7	6	A#7/Bb7
7	A7	7	F#7/Gb7	7	D7	7	B7
8	A#7/Bb7	8	G7	8	D#7/Eb7	8	C7
9	B7	9	G#7/Ab7	9	E7	9	C#7/Db7
10	C7	10	A7	10	F7	10	D7
11	C#7/Db7	11	A#7/Bb7	11	F#7/Gb7	11	D#7/Eb7
12	D7	12	B7	12	G7	12	E7

*n inversion of a chord refers to the same notes in a different sequence. ...e, root position has the root of the chord as its lowest tone; first ...rsion has the 3rd of the chord as the lowest note; second inversion has ... 5th of the chord as the lowest note; and third inversion has the 7th of ... chord as the lowest note

About the Chords

*I*t is not possible to include every chord in one book — there are just too many chords. Choices must be made in assembling any chord book.

In this book I have used the following criteria in selecting chords and chord forms for inclusion:

1. I have included all of the basic first position chords that beginners are likely to need.

2. I have included all of the most commonly used substitute and altered chords for each harmonic function.

3. I have included only chords in root position, except for the 7♭9 chord which has the ♭9th in the bass. Inversions can be derived without too much difficulty.

4. I have tried as much as possible to include one chord form with its root on the sixth string, one with its root on the fifth string, and one with its root on the fourth string for each chord. It was not always possible do this.

5. Where there are more than three movable forms for a chord type, I have tried to use all of them at one time or another. Thus, If you are looking for a particular chord (say G# Major seventh) you might try looking at the same type of chord (in this case Major sevenths) in other keys, and move any interesting chord forms you find up or down the neck to bring them into the desired key.

There are more chords listed in the tables than are diagrammed in chord frames. You can always use the tables of chord construction and the necessary note table to try to construct forms other than the ones given.

Also, you can have notes other than the root in the bass. This will alter the harmonic effect somewhat. (See the Psycho-acoustic Hierarchy Section on page 93) No matter how far apart the notes are, what sequence they are in, or how many times they are repeated — as long as at least one of each necessary note is present the chord retains its harmonic function.

There are many other chord forms possible. If you don't find it here, that doesn't mean that it doesn't exist, only that it is uncommon. A greater understanding of music theory and a better working knowledge of the fingerboard will help you to decipher whatever strange chords you may encounter, and even let you invent your own!

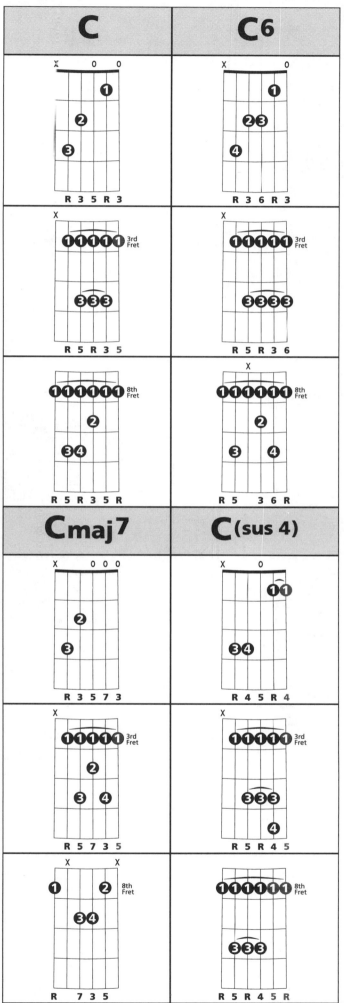

Root: C
Harmonic Function: Minor

Cmin

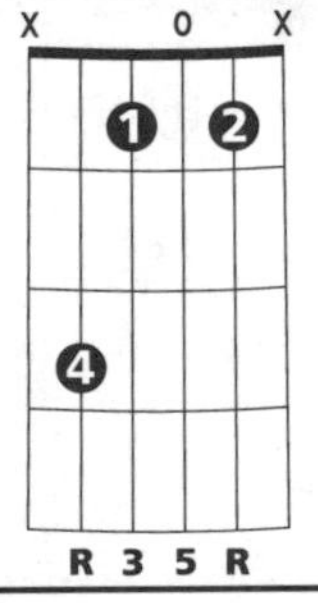

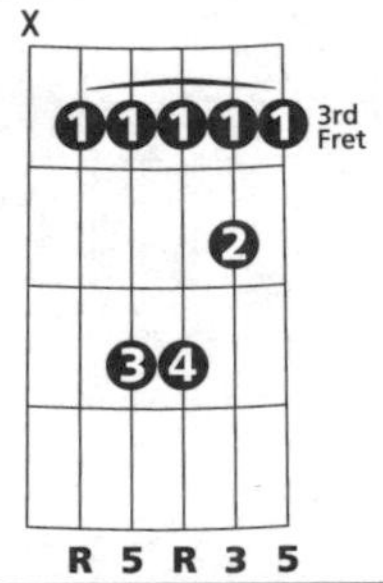

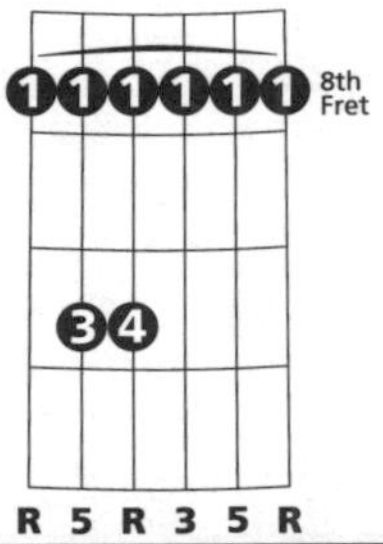

X   0   X

R 3 5 R

X

R 5 R 3 5   3rd Fret

R 5 R 3 5 R   8th Fret

Cmin6

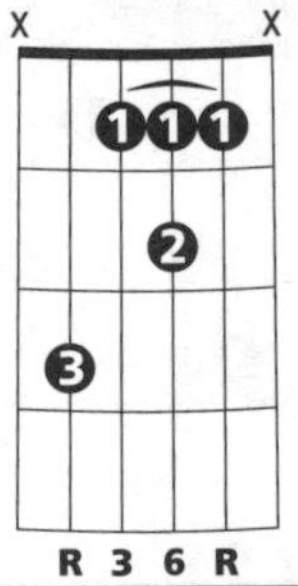

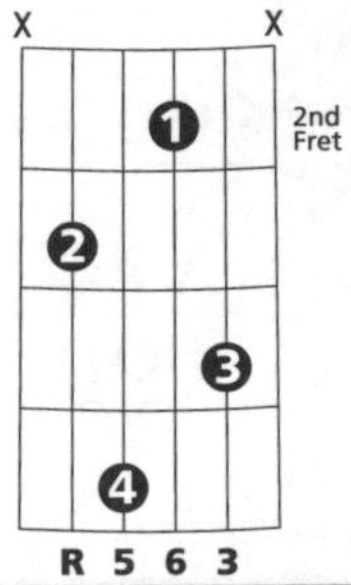

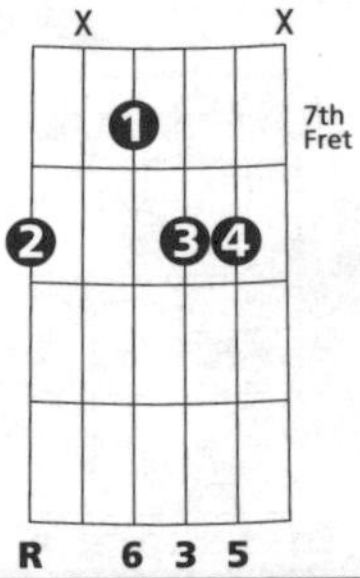

X   X

R 3 6 R

X   X

R 5 6 3   2nd Fret

X   X

R   6 3 5   7th Fret

Cmin7

X   X

R 3 7 R

X

R 5 7 3 5   3rd Fret

X

R 5 7 3 5 R   8th Fret

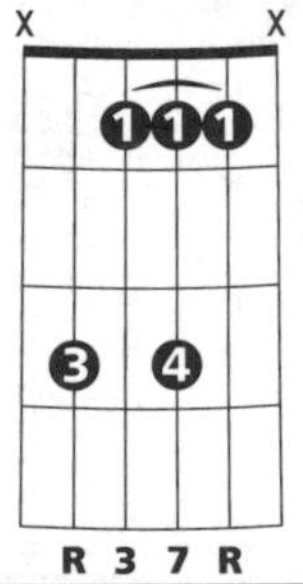

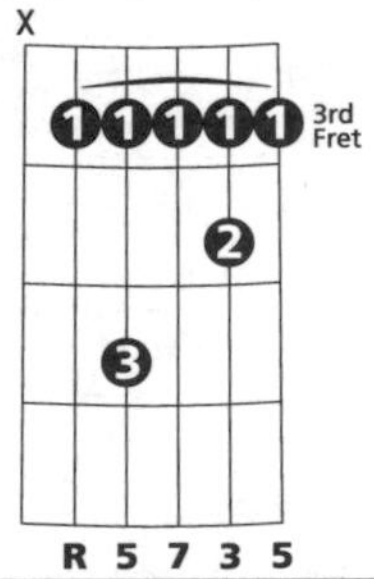

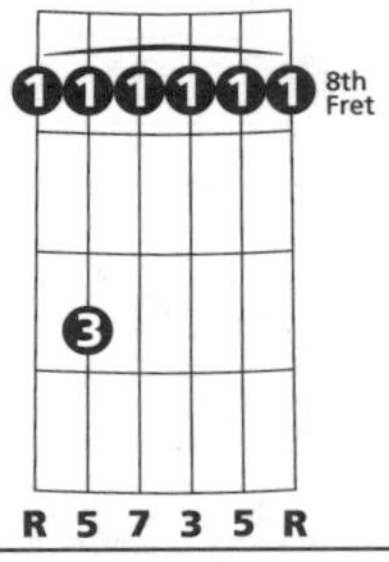

Cmin7-5

X

R 3 7 R 5

X   X

R 5 7 3   3rd Fret

X   X

R   7 3 5   7th Fret

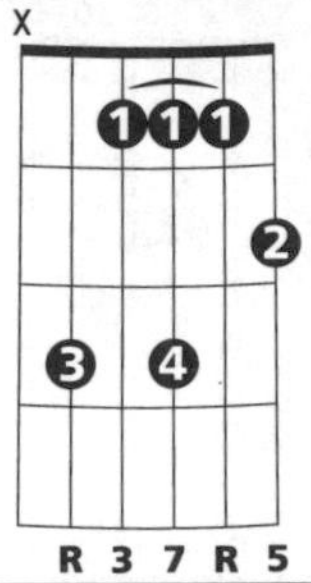

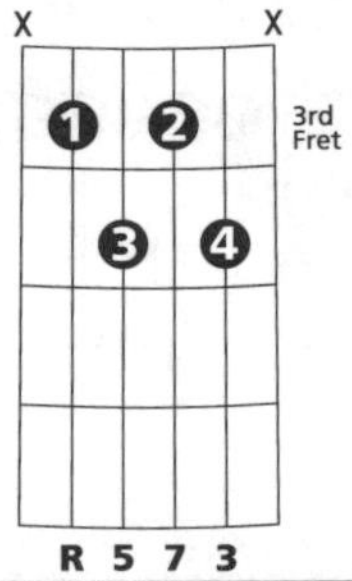

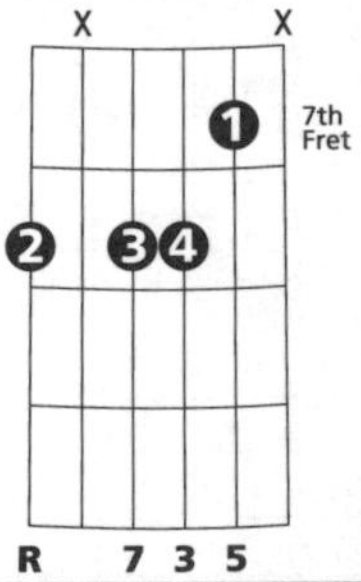

Root: C
Harmonic Function: Minor

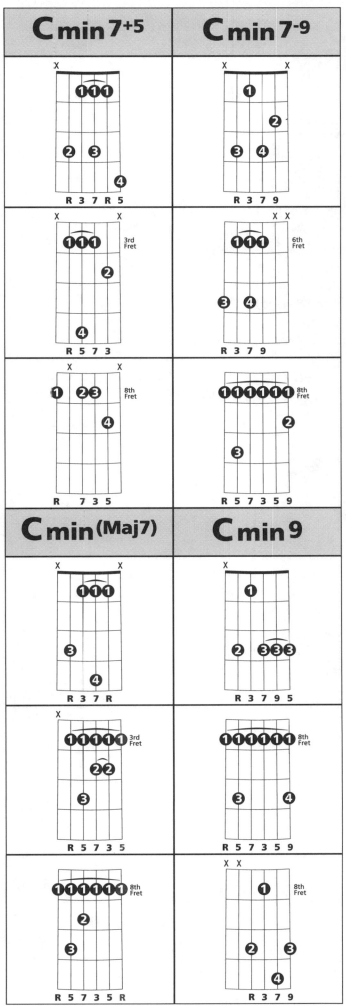

Cmin 7+5

X
R 3 7 R 5

3rd Fret
R 5 7 3

X   X
8th Fret
R   7 3 5

Cmin 7-9

X   X
R 3 7 9

X X
6th Fret
R 3 7 9

8th Fret
R 5 7 3 5 9

Cmin (Maj7)

X   X
R 3 7 R

3rd Fret
R 5 7 3 5

8th Fret
R 5 7 3 5 R

Cmin 9

X
R 3 7 9 5

8th Fret
R 5 7 3 5 9

X X
8th Fret
R 3 7 9

23

Root: C
Harmonic Function: Seventh

C7

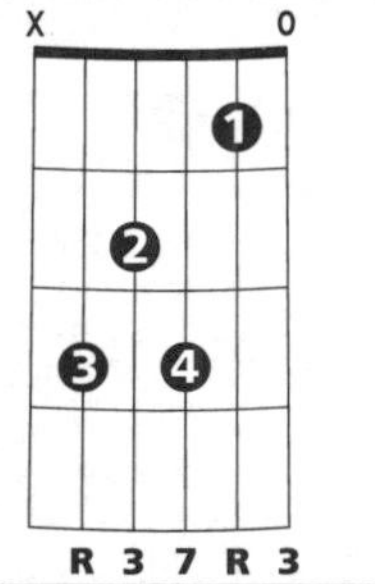

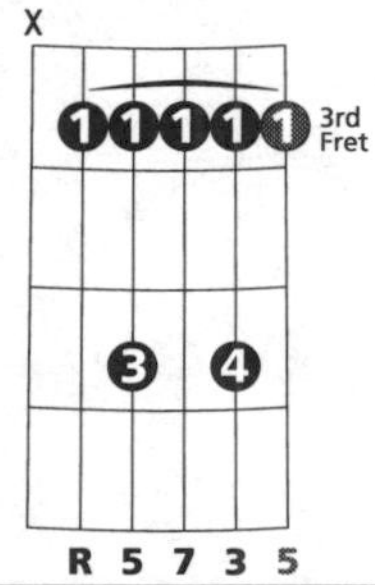

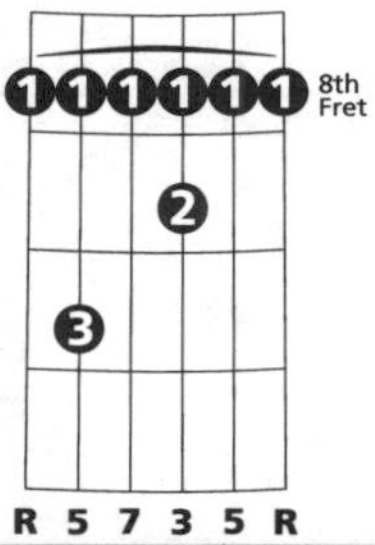

R 3 7 R 3

3rd Fret

R 5 7 3 5

8th Fret

R 5 7 3 5 R

C+

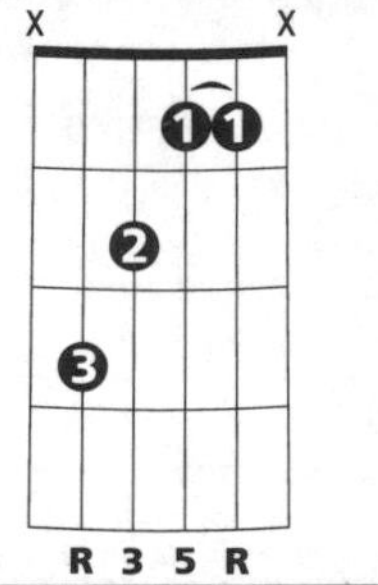

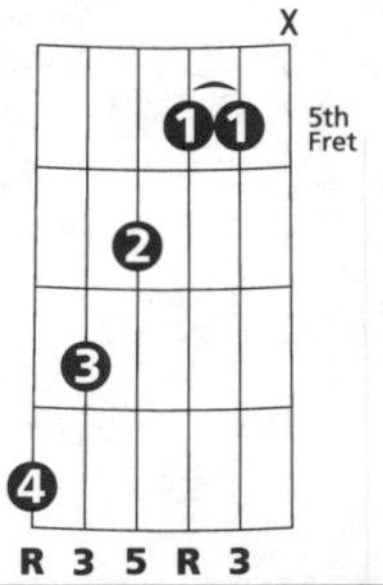

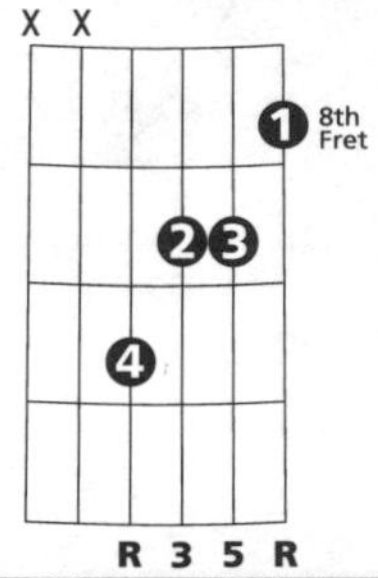

R 3 5 R

5th Fret

R 3 5 R 3

8th Fret

R 3 5 R

C7(sus 4)

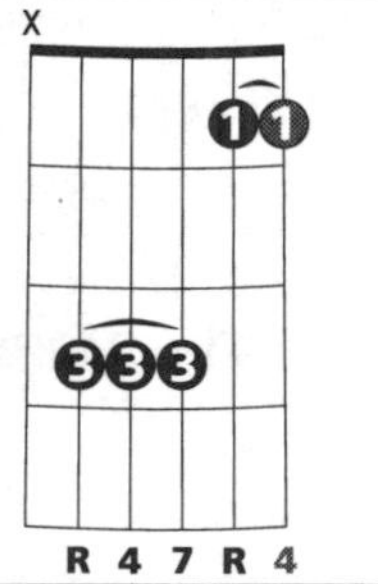

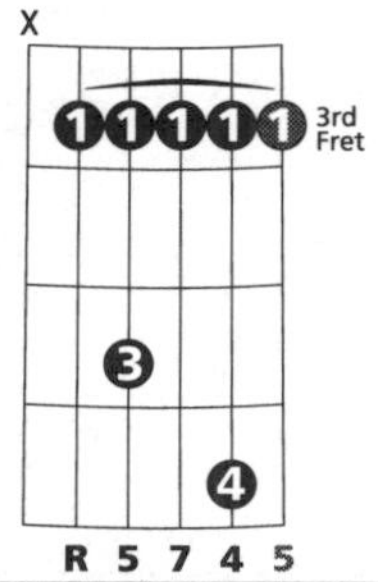

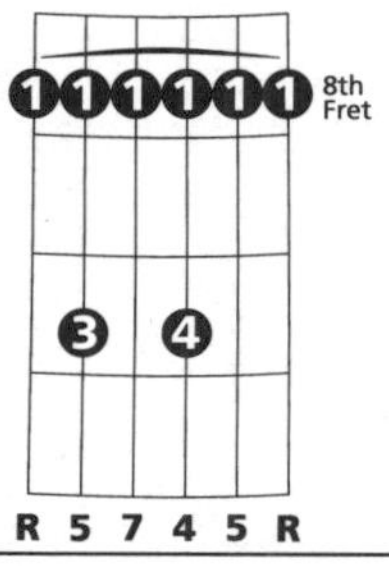

R 4 7 R 4

3rd Fret

R 5 7 4 5

8th Fret

R 5 7 4 5 R

C7-5

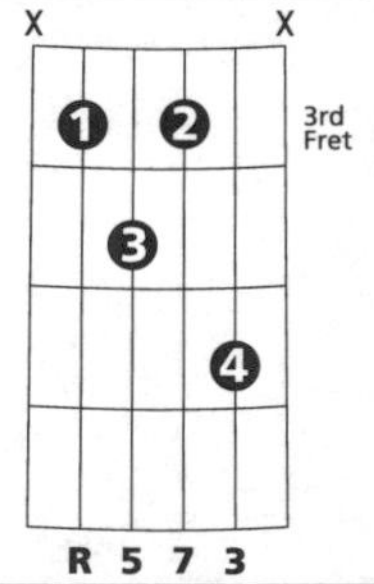

3rd Fret

R 5 7 3

8th Fret

R 5 7 3

7th Fret

R 7 3 5

24

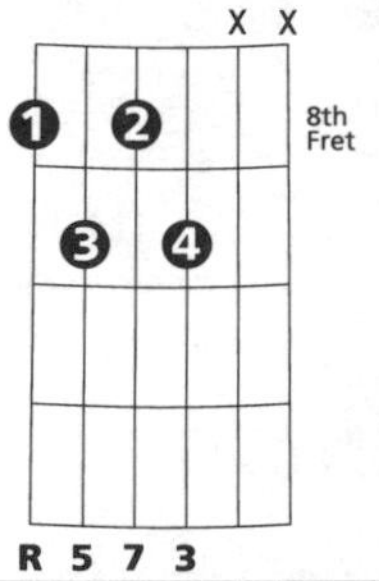

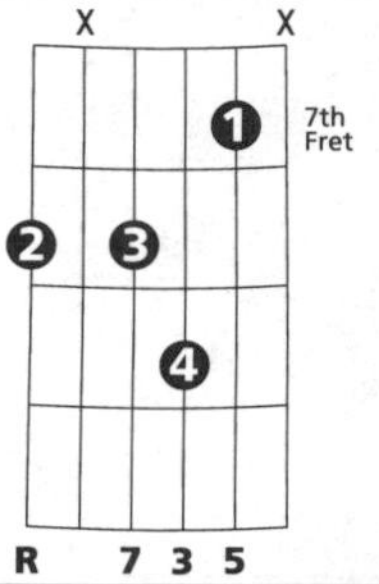

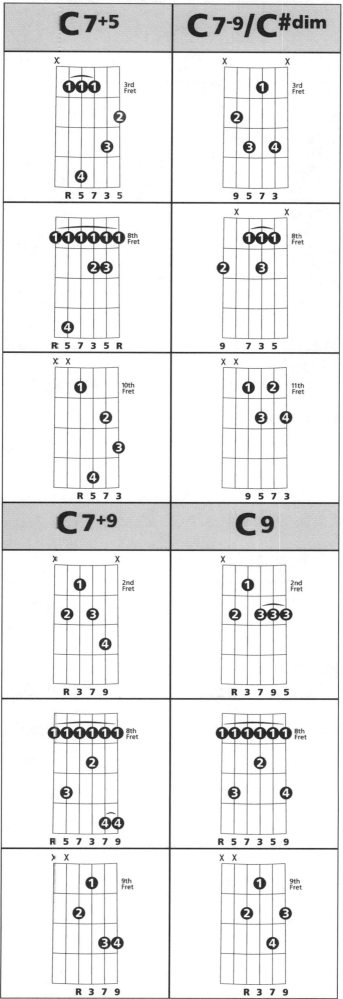

C7+5

C7-9/C#dim

C7+9

C9

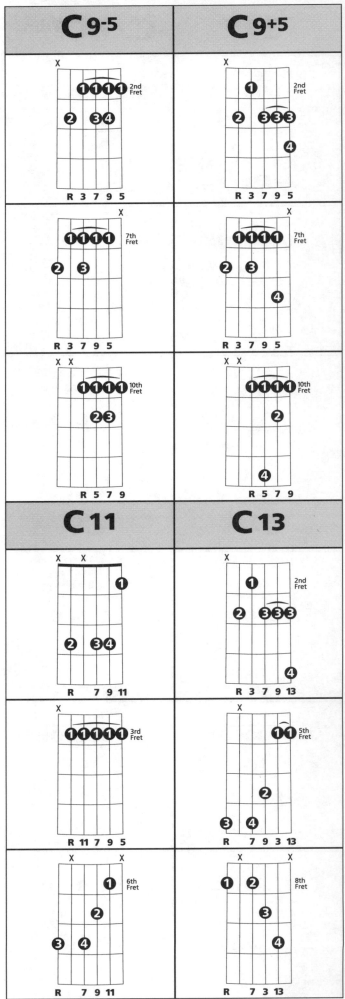

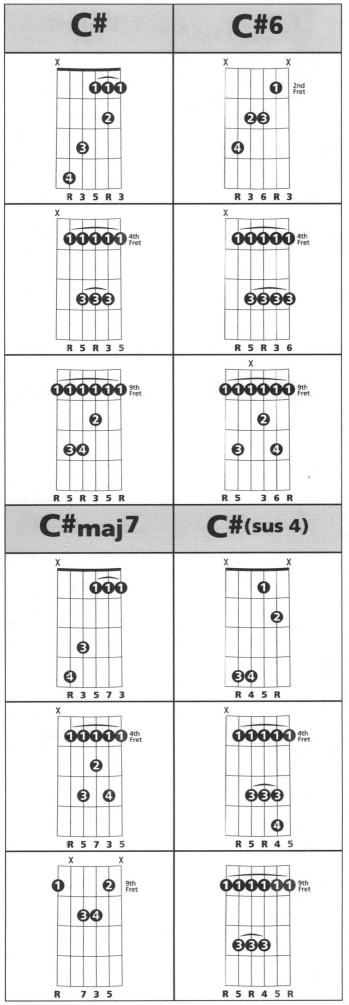

27

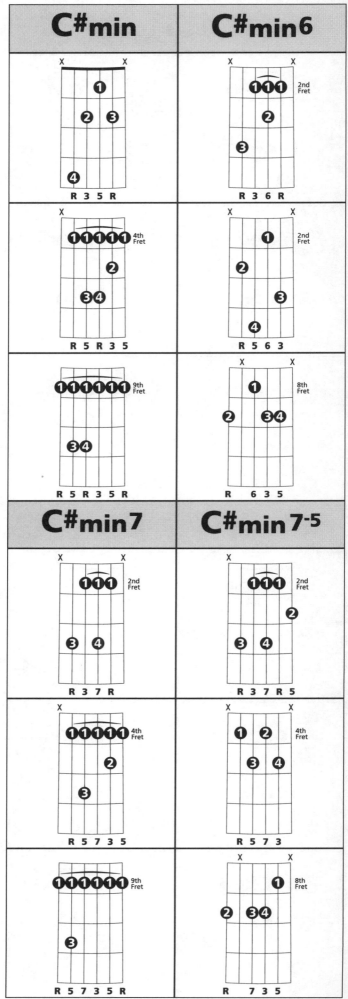

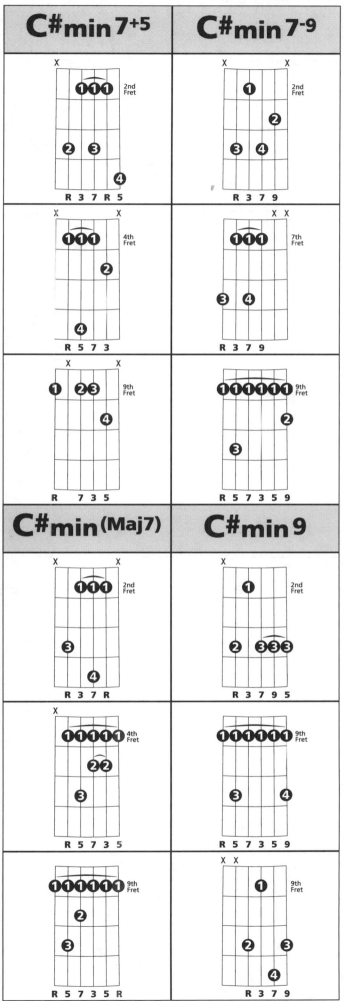

C#min 7+5

R 3 7 R 5

R 5 7 3

R 7 3 5

C#min 7-9

R 3 7 9

R 3 7 9

R 5 7 3 5 9

C#min (Maj7)

R 3 7 R

R 5 7 3 5

R 5 7 3 5 R

C#min 9

R 3 7 9 5

R 5 7 3 5 9

R 3 7 9

29

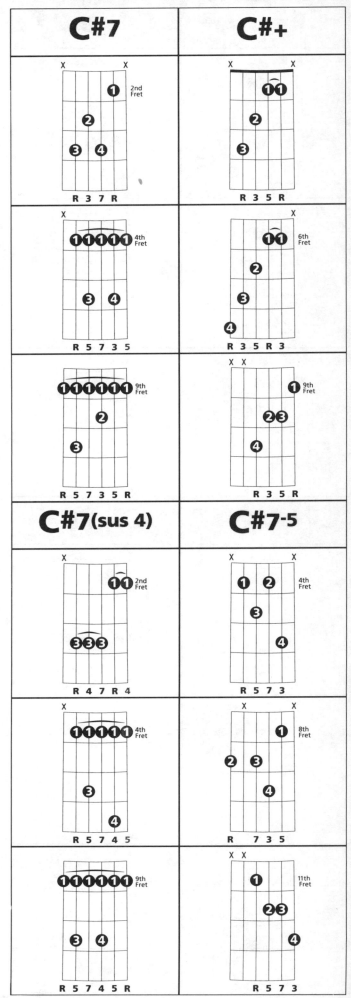

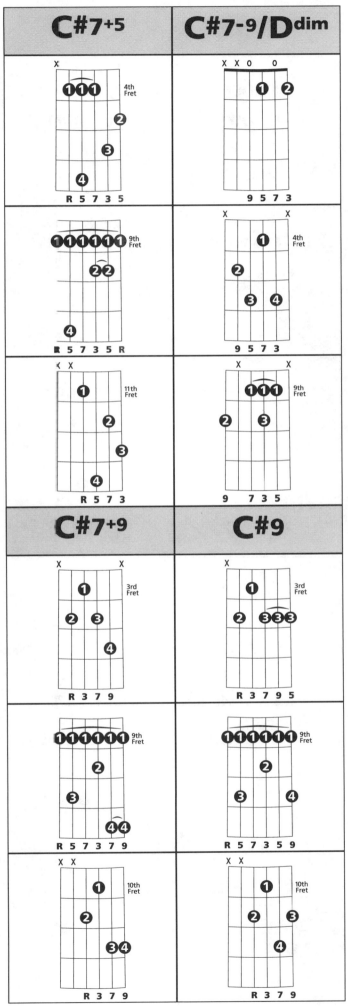

Root: C#
Harmonic Function: Seventh

C#9-5

C#9+5

C#11

C#13

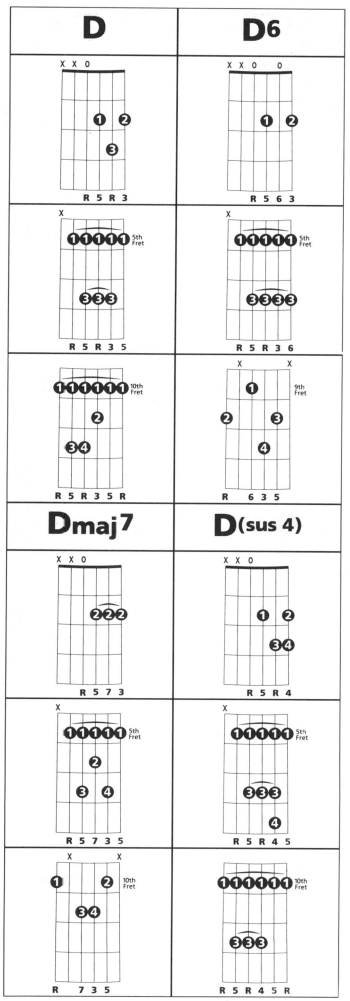

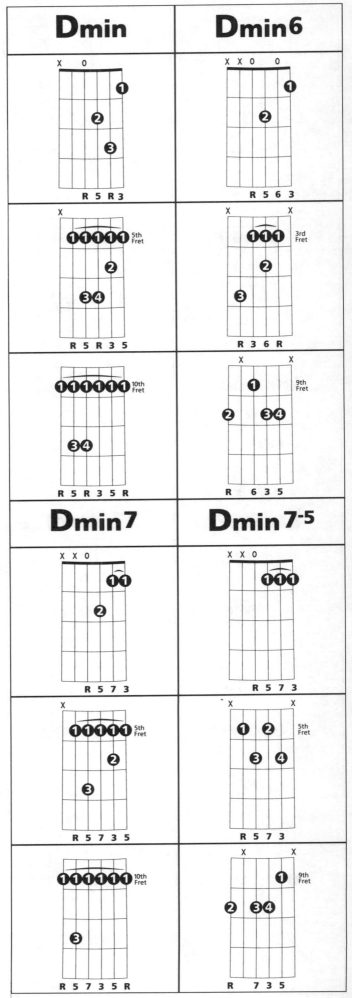

Root: D
Harmonic Function: Minor

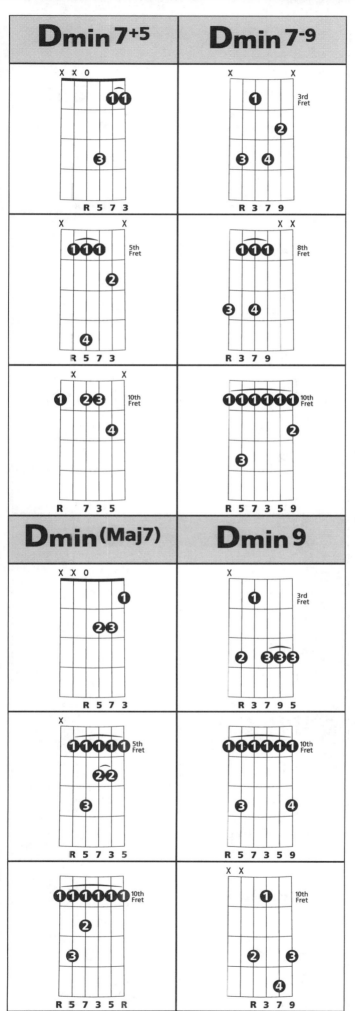

Dmin7+5

Dmin7-9

Dmin(Maj7)

Dmin9

35

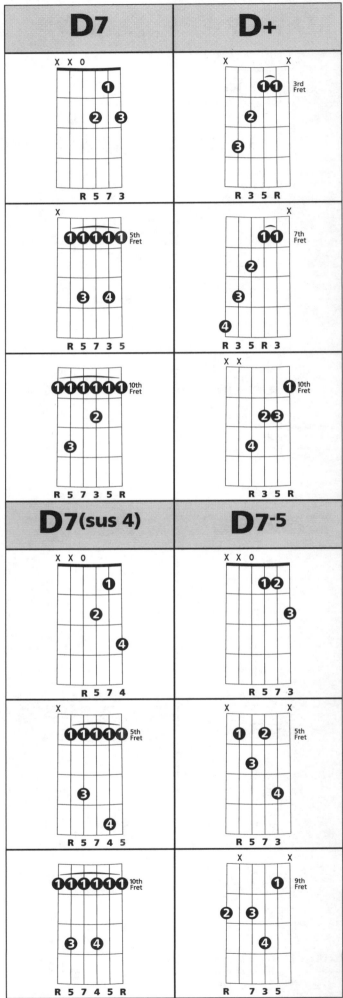

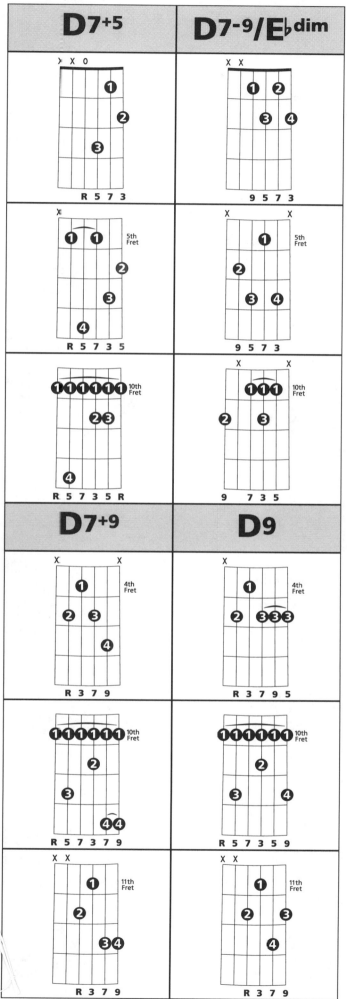

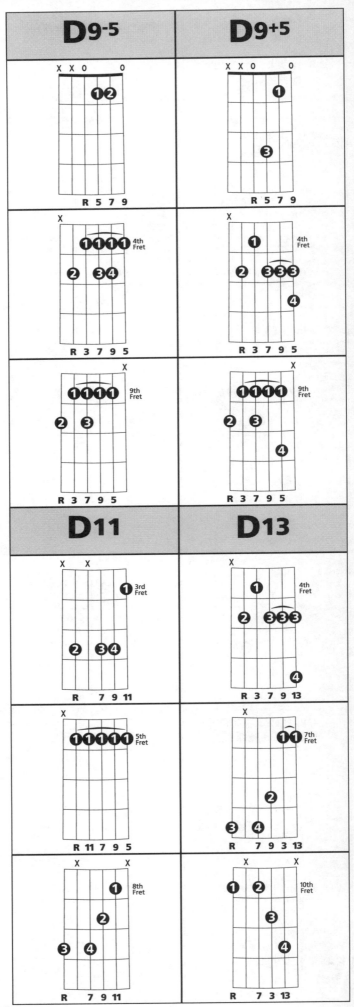

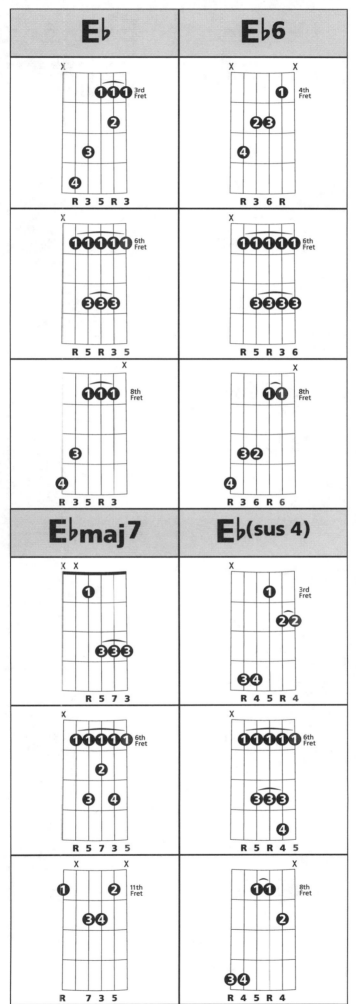

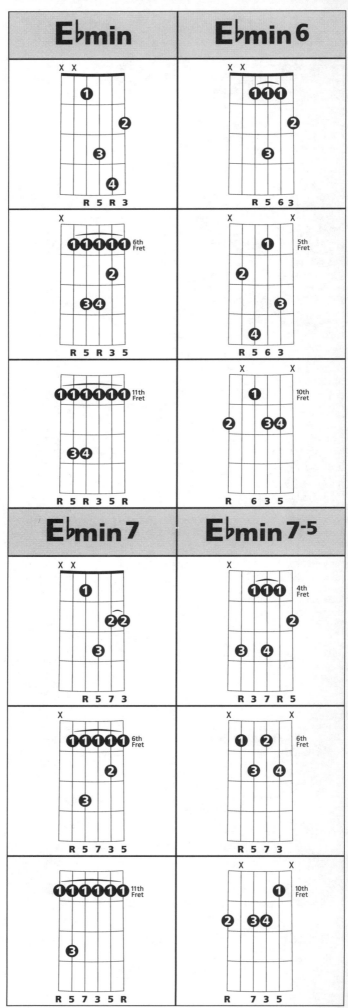

40

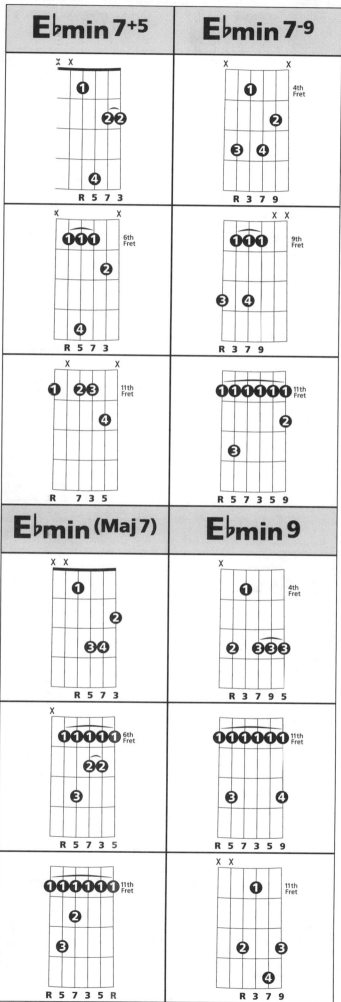

41

Root: E♭
Harmonic Function: Seventh

E♭7

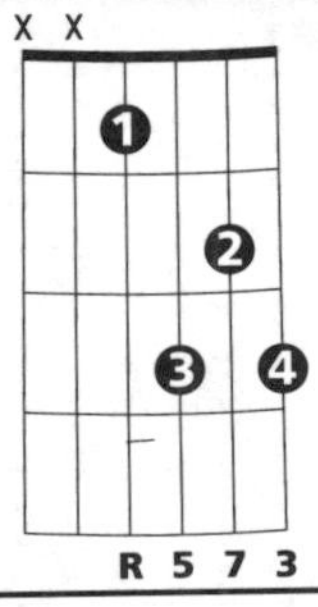
X X
R 5 7 3

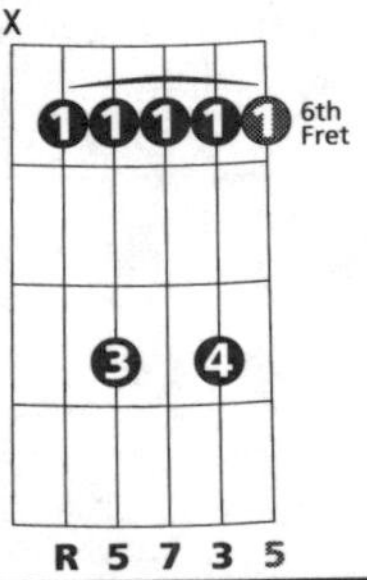
X
6th Fret
R 5 7 3 5

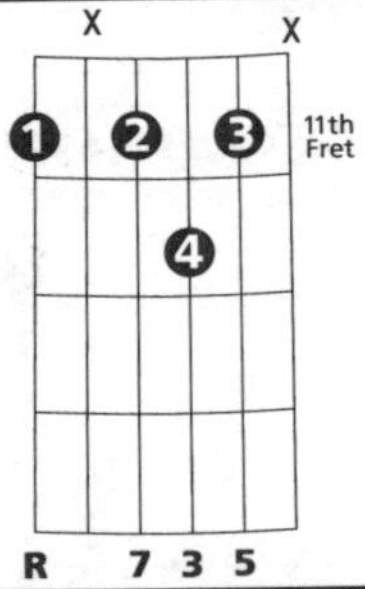
X X
11th Fret
R 7 3 5

E♭+

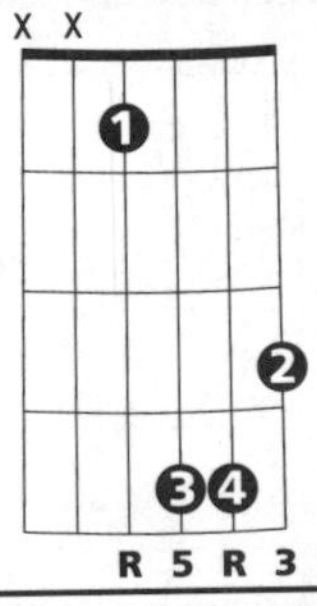
X X
R 5 R 3

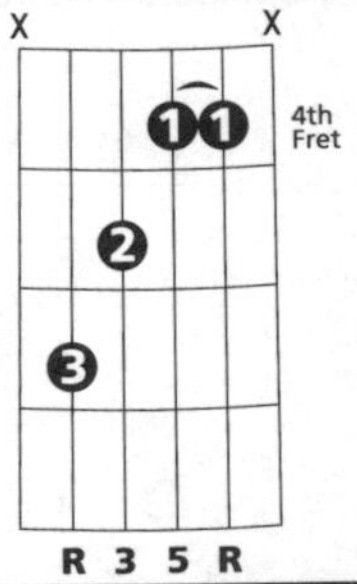
X X
4th Fret
R 3 5 R

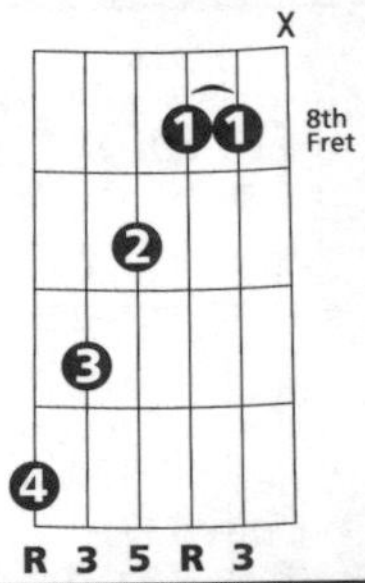
X
8th Fret
R 3 5 R 3

E♭7(sus 4)

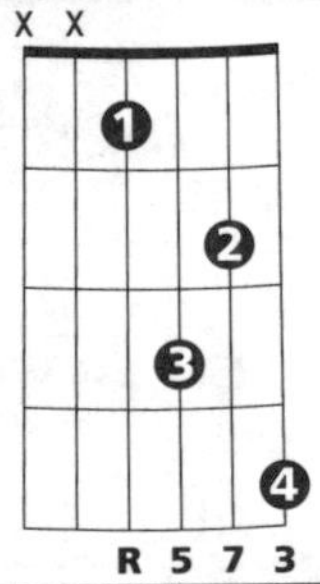
X X
R 5 7 3

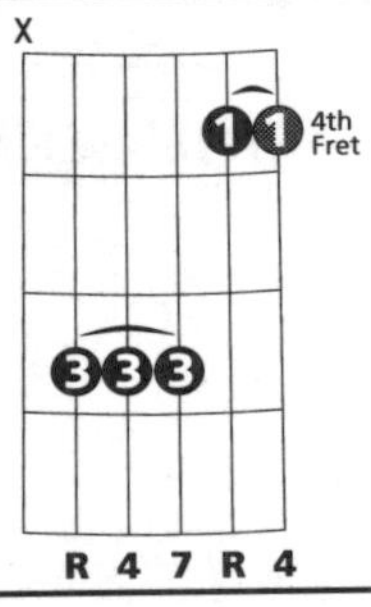
X
4th Fret
R 4 7 R 4

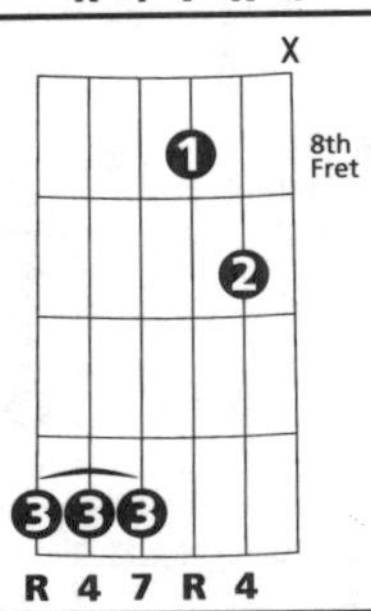
X
8th Fret
R 4 7 R 4

E♭7-5

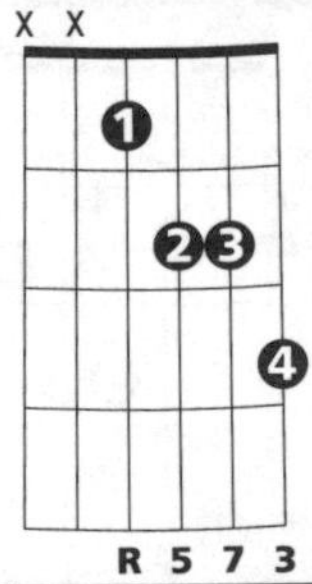
X X
R 5 7 3

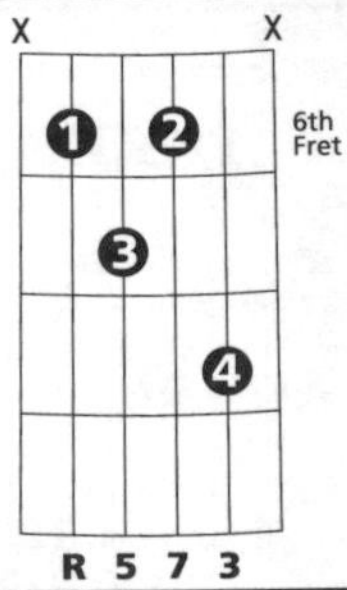
X X
6th Fret
R 5 7 3

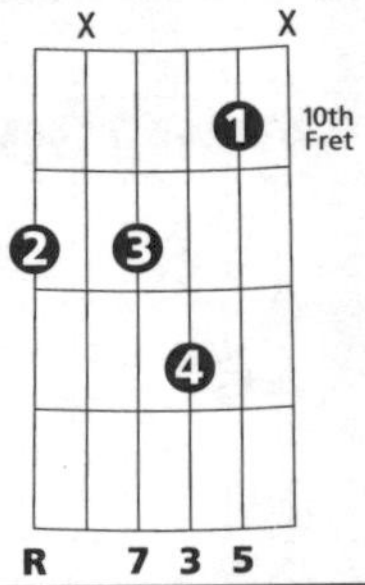
X X
10th Fret
R 7 3 5

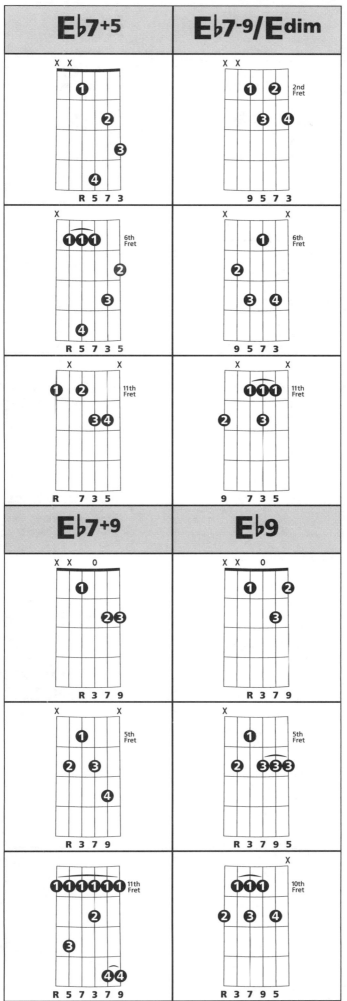

43

E♭9-5

X X
① ① ① ①
② ③
R 5 7 9

X
① ① ① ① 5th Fret
② ③ ④
R 3 7 9 5

X
① ① ① ① 10th Fret
② ③
R 3 7 9 5

E♭9+5

X X
① ① ① ①
②
④
R 5 7 9

X
① 5th Fret
② ③ ③ ③
④
R 3 7 9 5

X
① ① ① ① 10th Fret
② ③
④
R 3 7 9 5

E♭11

X X
① 4th Fret
② ③ ④
R 7 9 11

X
① ① ① ① ① 6th Fret
R 11 7 9 5

X X
① 9th Fret
②
③ ④
R 7 9 11

E♭13

X
① 5th Fret
② ③ ③ ③
④
R 3 7 9 13

X
① ① 8th Fret
②
③ ④
R 7 9 3 13

X X
① ② 11th Fret
③
④
R 7 3 13

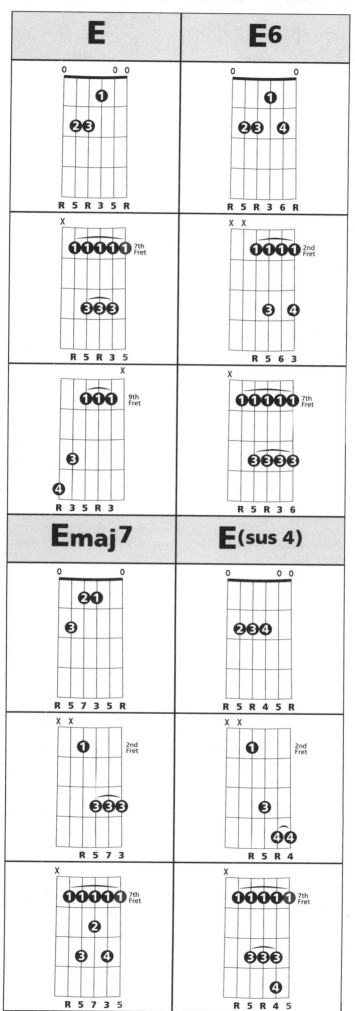

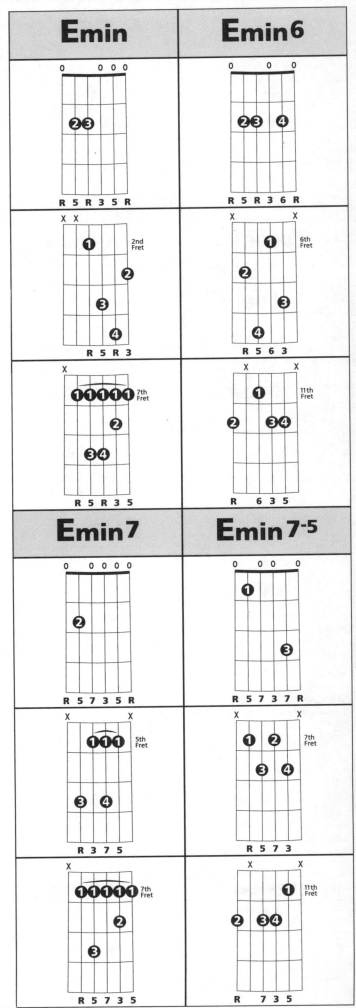

Emin	Emin6

R 5 R 3 5 R	R 5 R 3 6 R
R 5 R 3 (2nd Fret)	R 5 6 3 (6th Fret)
R 5 R 3 5 (7th Fret)	R 6 3 5 (11th Fret)

Emin7	Emin7-5

R 5 7 3 5 R	R 5 7 3 7 R
R 3 7 5 (5th Fret)	R 5 7 3 (7th Fret)
R 5 7 3 5 (7th Fret)	R 7 3 5 (11th Fret)

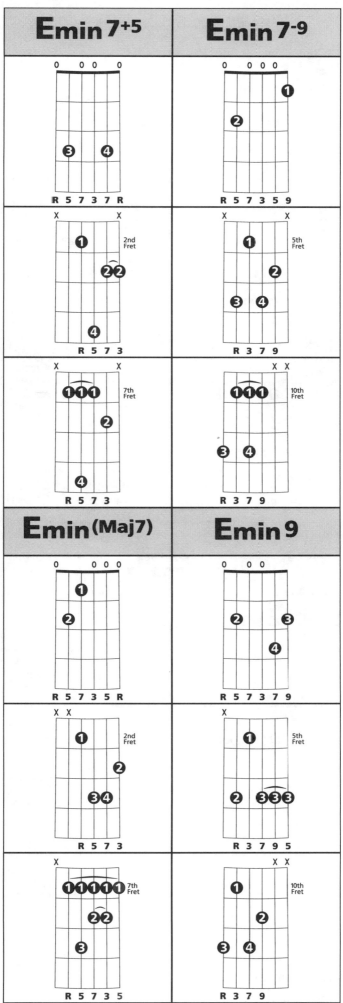

Root: E
Harmonic Function: Seventh

E7

R 5 7 3 7 R

R 3 7 R — 5th Fret

R 5 7 3 5 — 7th Fret

E+

R 5 R 3 5 R

R 3 5 R — 5th Fret

R 3 5 R 3 — 9th Fret

E7(sus 4)

R 5 7 4 5 R

R 5 7 4 5 — 7th Fret

R 4 7 R 4 — 9th Fret

E7-5

R 5 7 3 7 R

R 5 7 3 — 7th Fret

R 7 3 5 — 11th Fret

Root: E
Harmonic Function: Seventh

E7+5	**E7-9/Fdim**

E7+5

0 0 0

①②
④

R 5 7 3 5 R

X X

① 2nd Fret
②
③
④

R 5 7 3

X

①①① 7th Fret
②
③
④

R 5 7 3 5

E7-9/Fdim

X 0   0 X

① ②

9 7 3 5

X X

① ② 3rd Fret
③ ④

9 5 7 3

X   X

① 7th Fret
②
③ ④

9 5 7 3

E7+9	**E9**

E7+9

0   0

①
②
③④

R 5 7 3 7 9

X X

①
②
③④

R 3 7 9

X   X

① 6th. Fret
② ③
④

R 3 7 9

E9

0 0 0

①
②   ③

R 5 7 3 5 9

X

① 6th Fret
② ③③③

R 3 7 9 5

X

①①① 11th Fret
② ③ ④

R 3 7 9 5

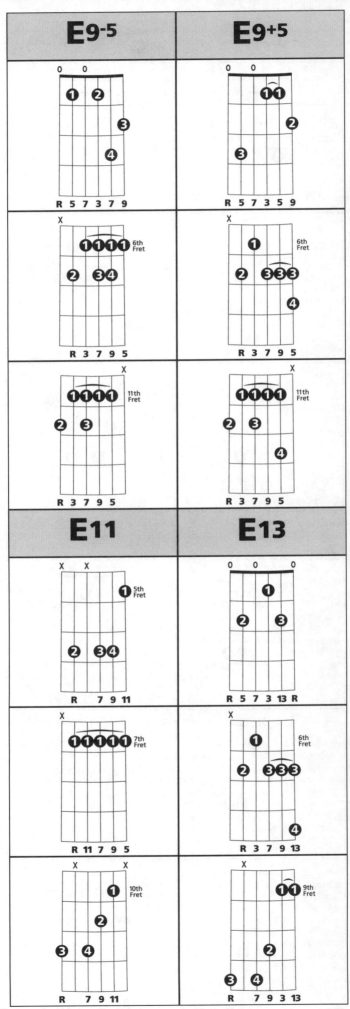

E9-5

E9+5

E11

E13

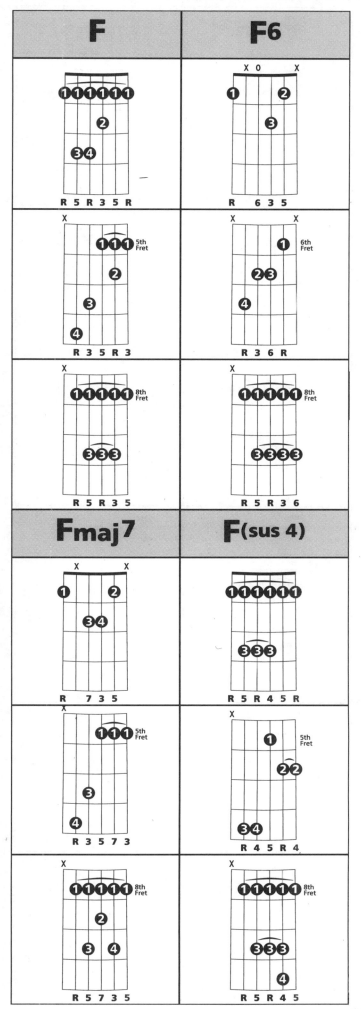

Root: F
Harmonic Function: Minor

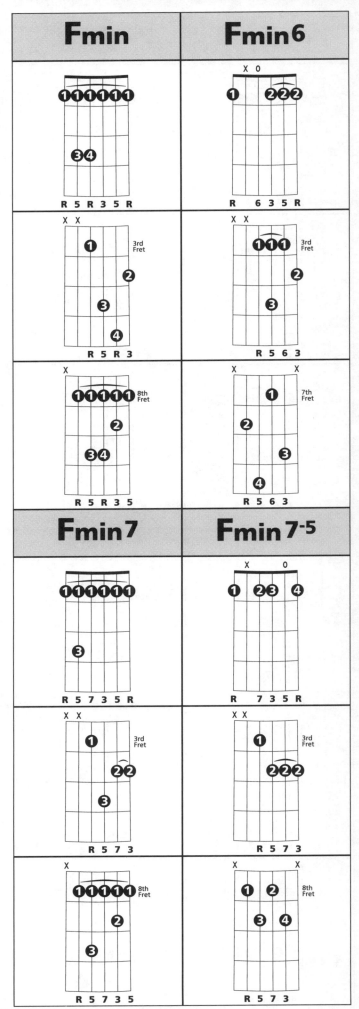

Fmin

Fmin6

Fmin7

Fmin7⁻⁵

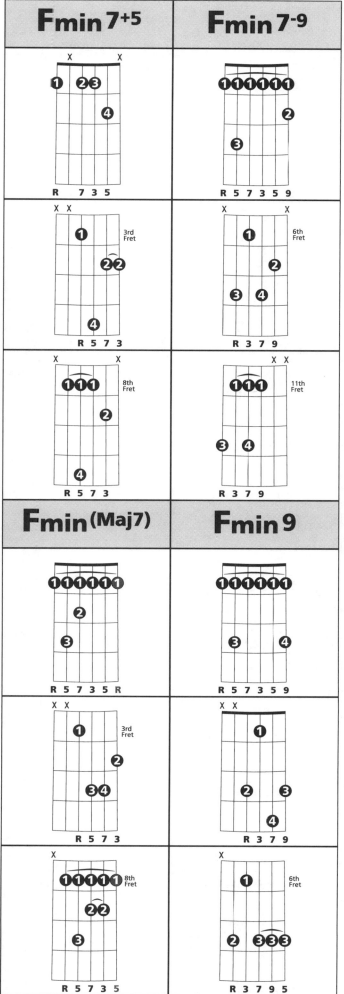

Root: F
Harmonic Function: Seventh

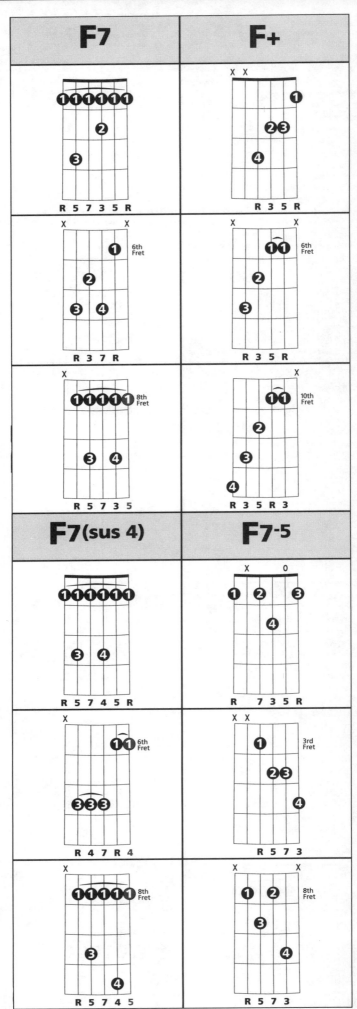

F7	F+

F7 diagrams:
- R 5 7 3 5 R
- R 3 7 R (6th Fret)
- R 5 7 3 5 (8th Fret)

F+ diagrams:
- R 3 5 R
- R 3 5 R (6th Fret)
- R 3 5 R 3 (10th Fret)

F7(sus 4)	F7-5

F7(sus 4) diagrams:
- R 5 7 4 5 R
- R 4 7 R 4 (6th Fret)
- R 5 7 4 5 (8th Fret)

F7-5 diagrams:
- R 7 3 5 R
- R 5 7 3 (3rd Fret)
- R 5 7 3 (8th Fret)

F7+5

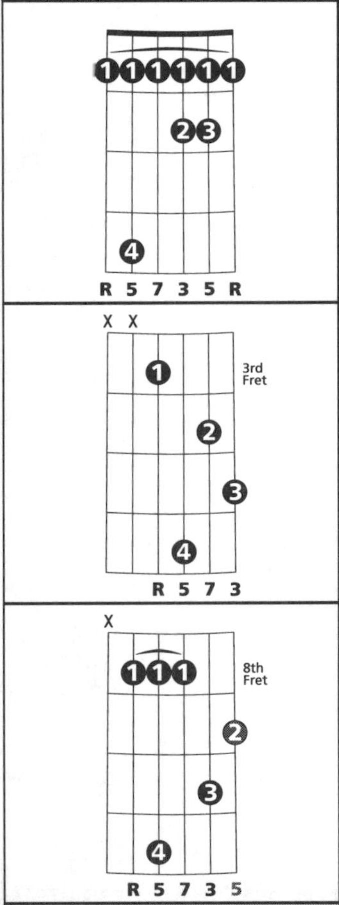

R 5 7 3 5 R

X X

3rd Fret

R 5 7 3

X

8th Fret

R 5 7 3 5

F7-9/F#dim

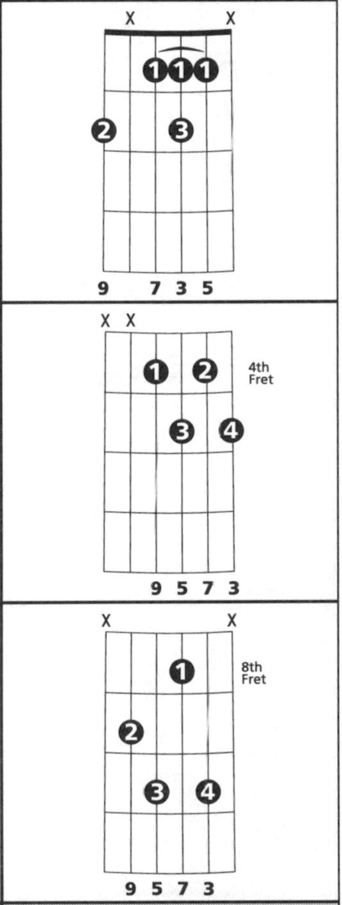

X   X

9 7 3 5

X X

4th Fret

9 5 7 3

X   X

8th Fret

9 5 7 3

F7+9

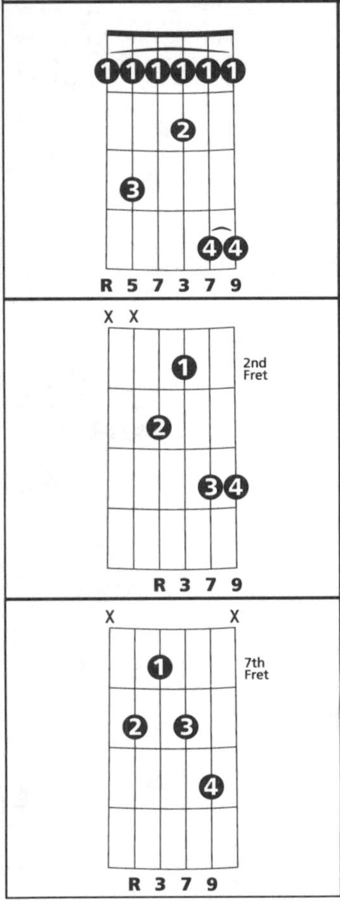

R 5 7 3 7 9

X X

2nd Fret

R 3 7 9

X   X

7th Fret

R 3 7 9

F9

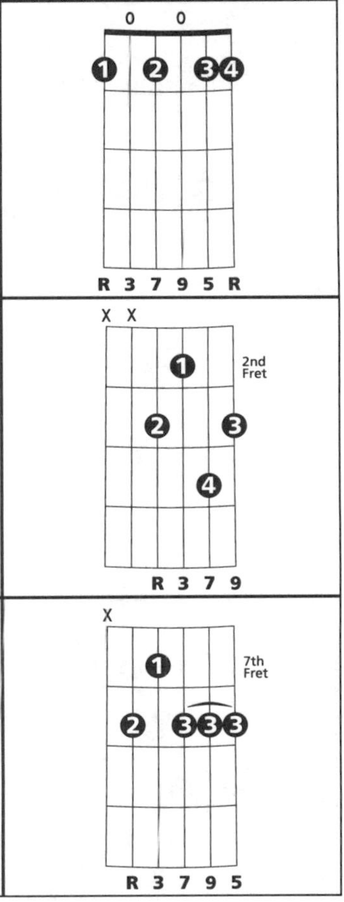

0   0

R 3 7 9 5 R

X X

2nd Fret

R 3 7 9

X

7th Fret

R 3 7 9 5

Root: F
Harmonic Function: Seventh

F9-5

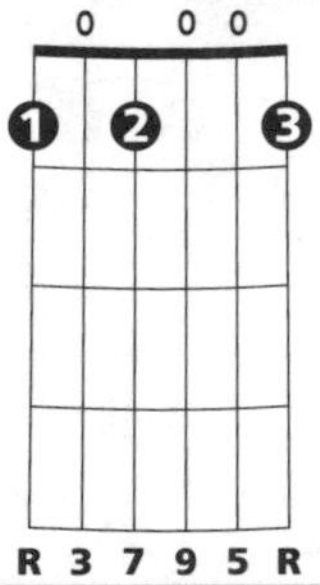

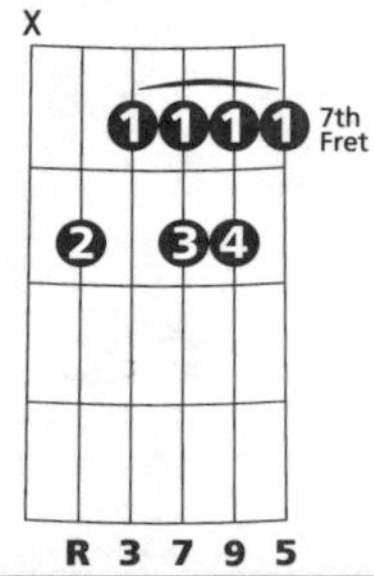

R 3 7 9 5 R

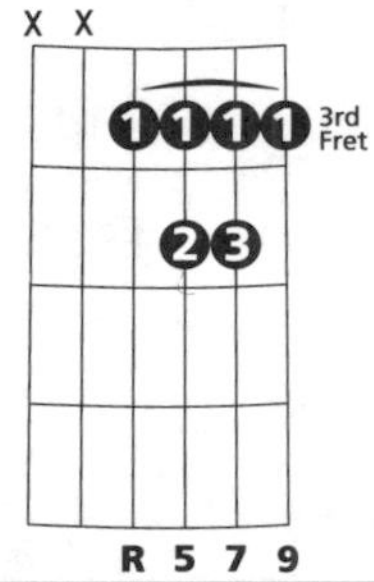

R 5 7 9

R 3 7 9 5

F9+5

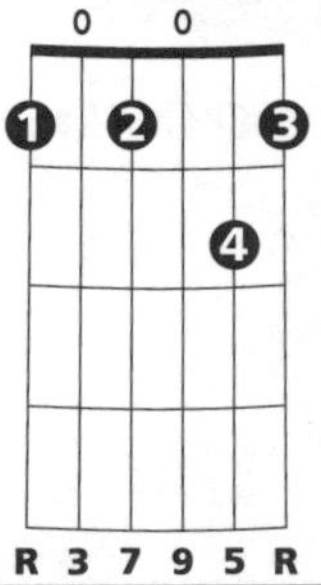

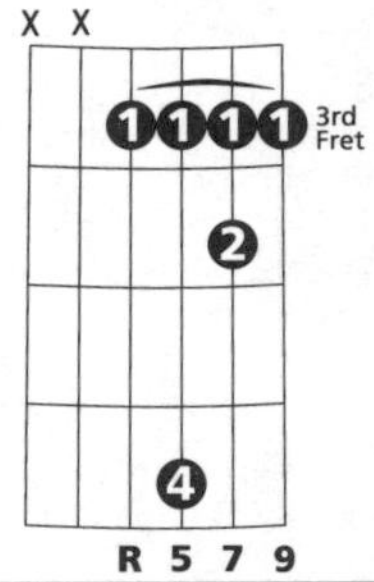

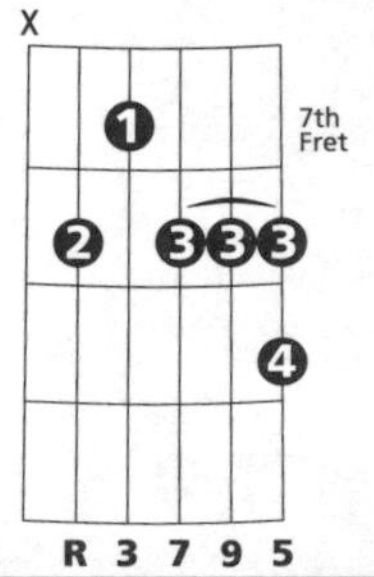

R 3 7 9 5 R

R 5 7 9

R 3 7 9 5

F11

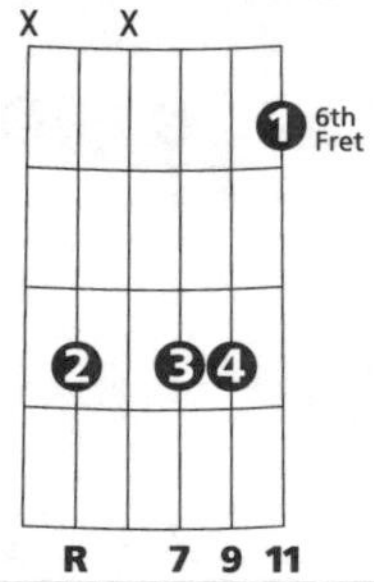

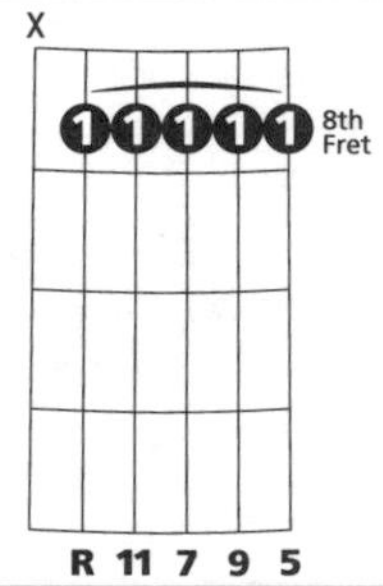

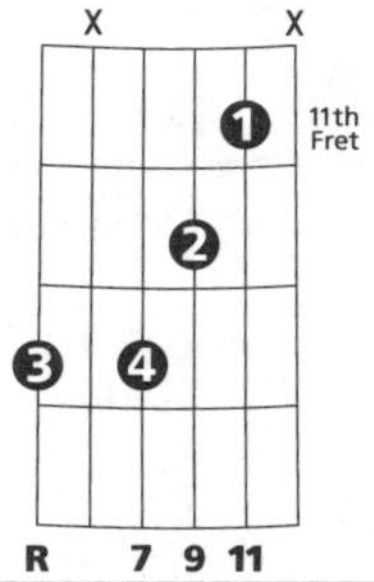

R 7 9 11

R 11 7 9 5

R 7 9 11

F13

R 7 3 13

R 3 7 9 13

R 7 9 3 13

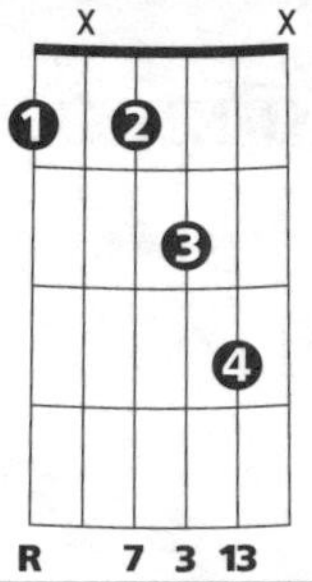

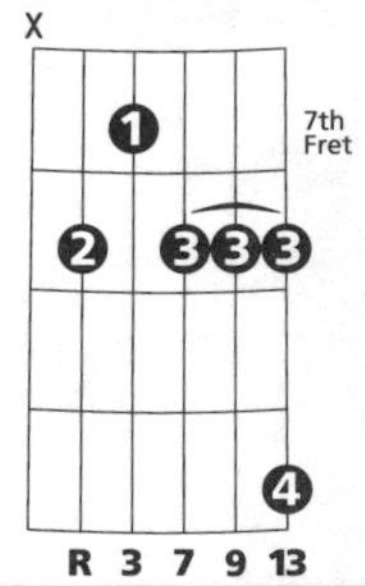

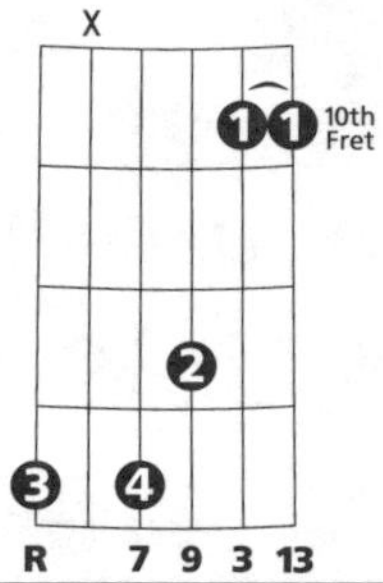

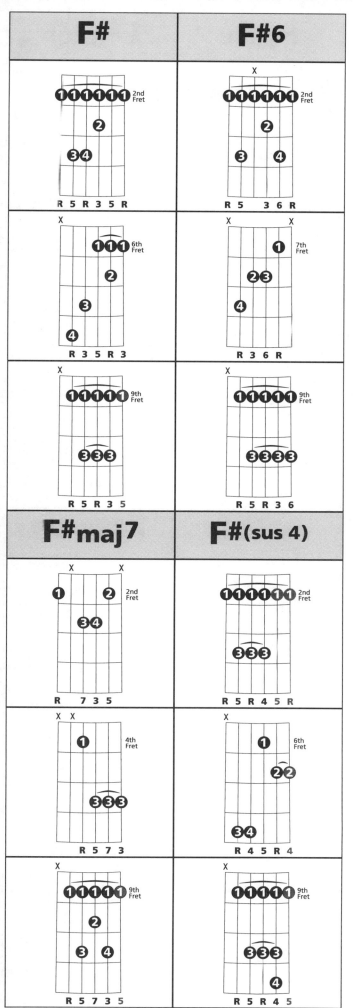

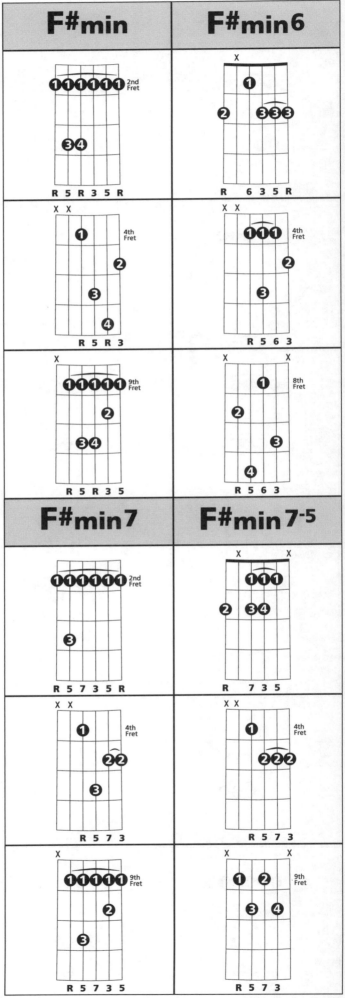

Root: F#
Harmonic Function: Minor

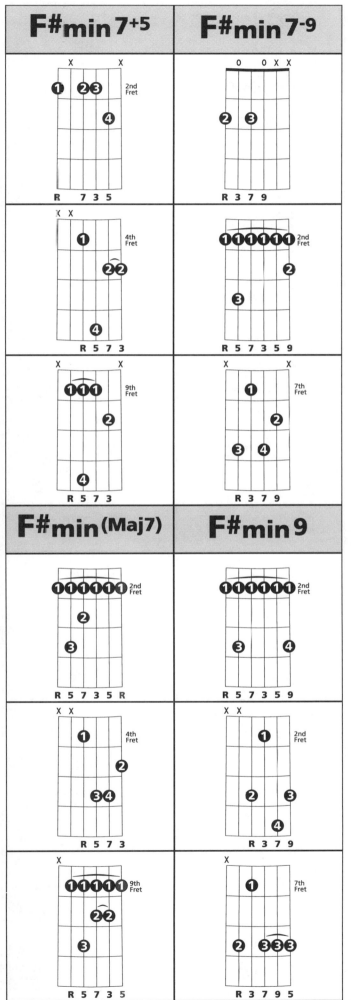

F#min 7+5   **F#min 7-9**

F#min (Maj7)   **F#min 9**

59

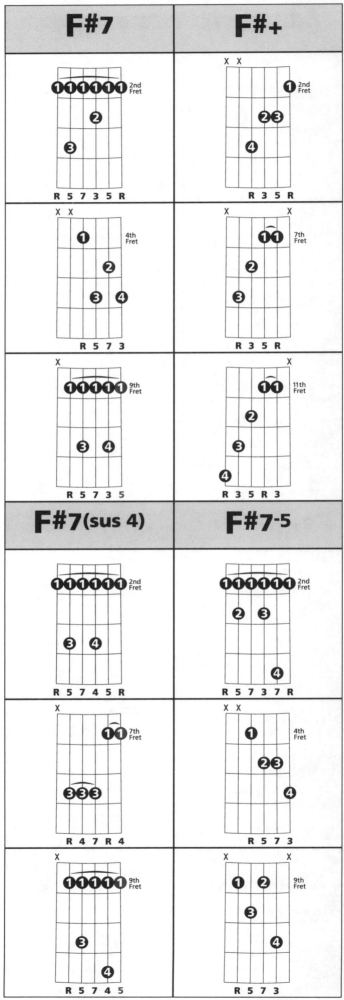

F#7 · **F#+** · **F#7(sus 4)** · **F#7-5**

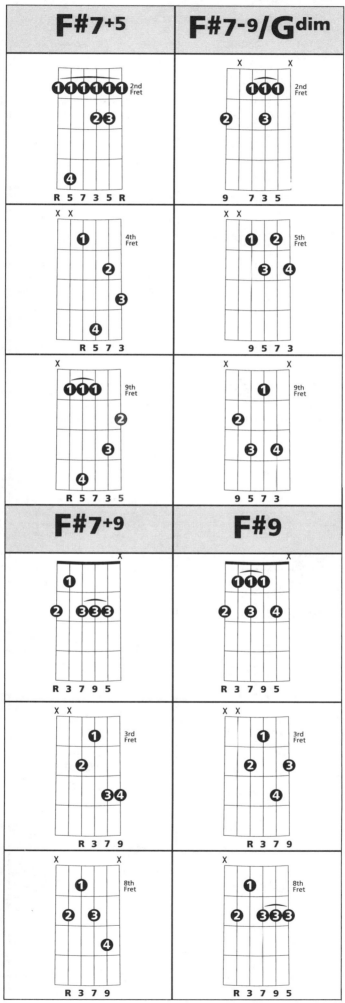

Root: F#
Harmonic Function: Seventh

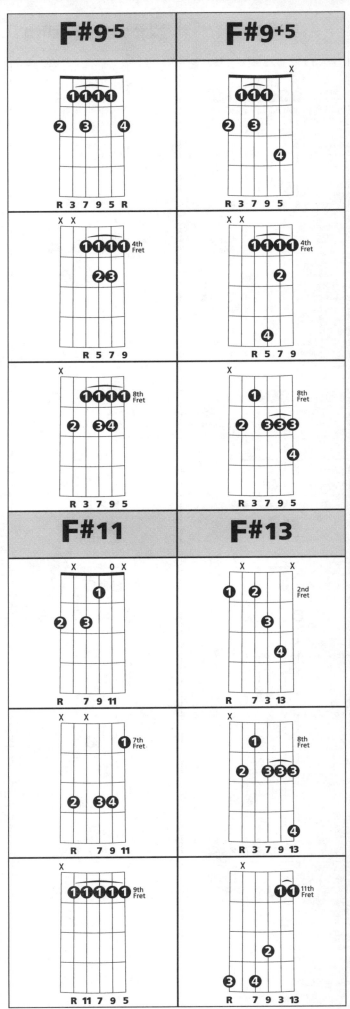

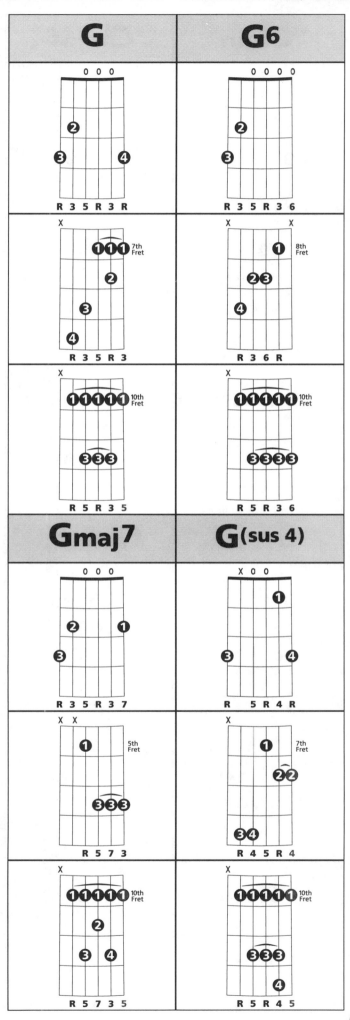

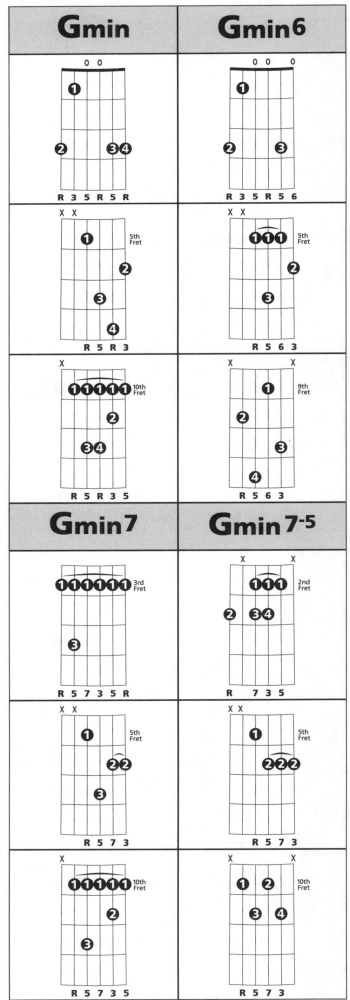

Root: G
Harmonic Function: Minor

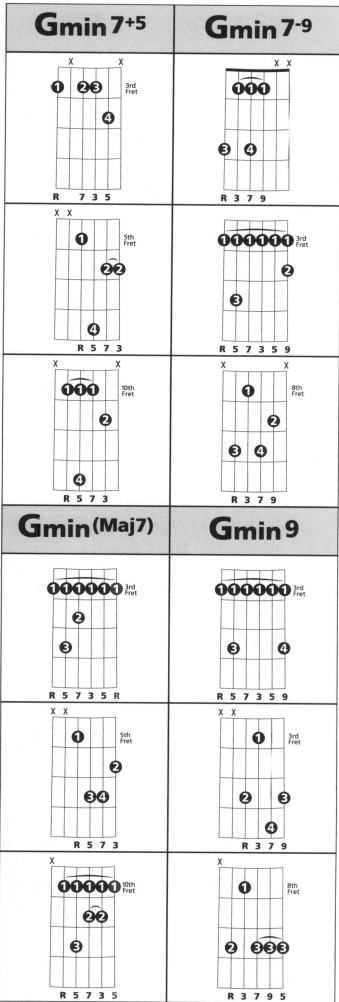

Gmin 7+5	Gmin 7-9

Gmin (Maj7) | **Gmin 9**

Root: G
Harmonic Function: Seventh

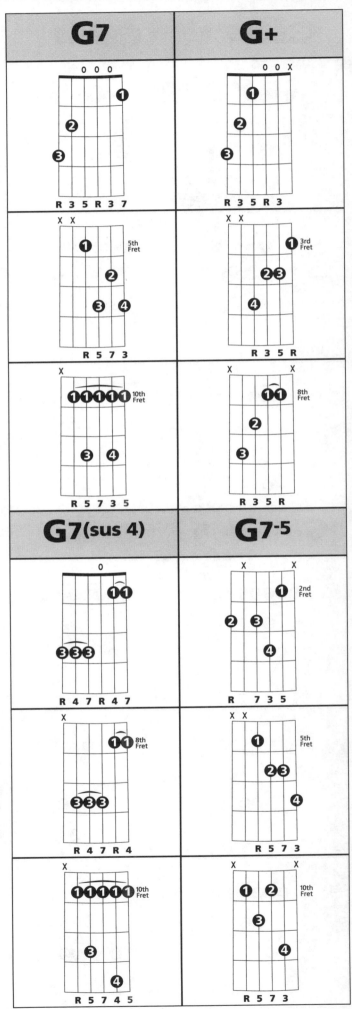

G7

G+

G7(sus 4)

G7⁻5

66

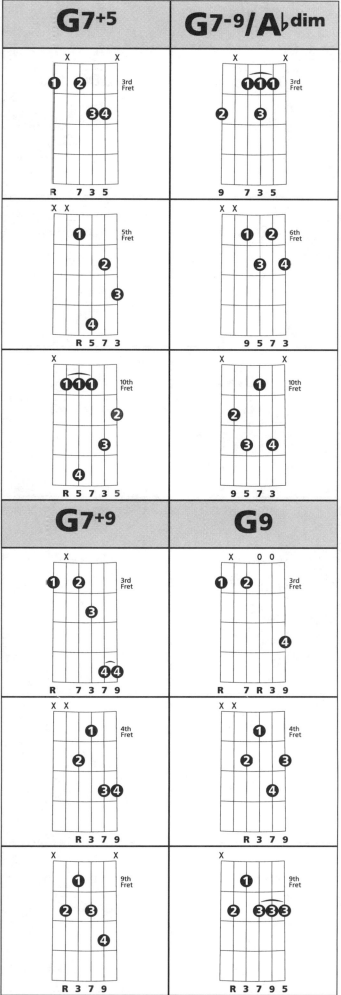

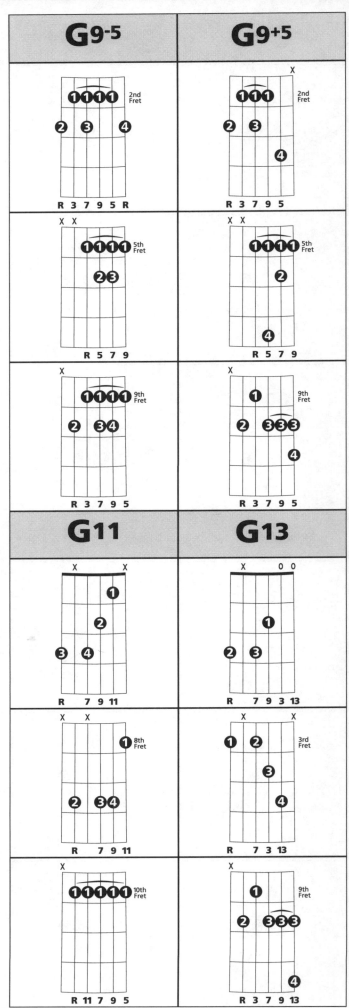

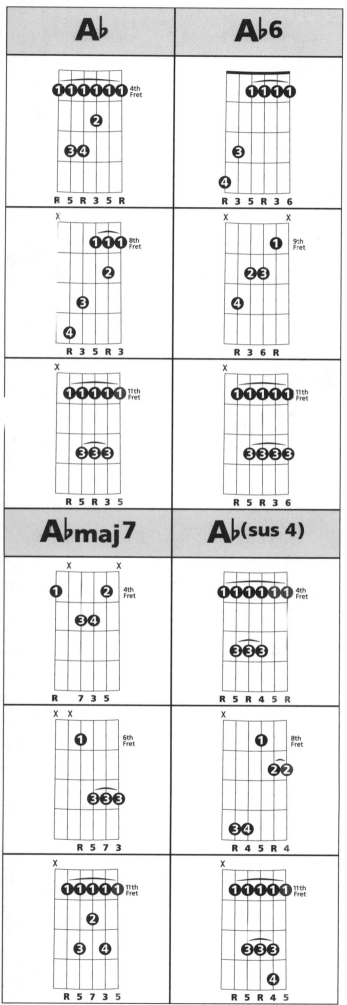

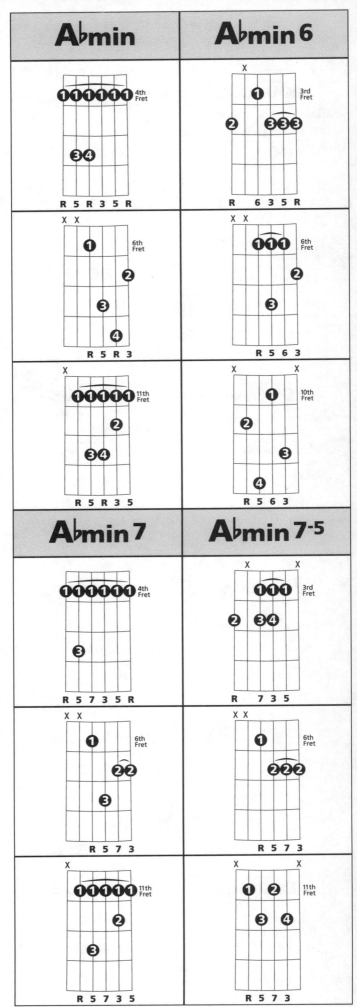

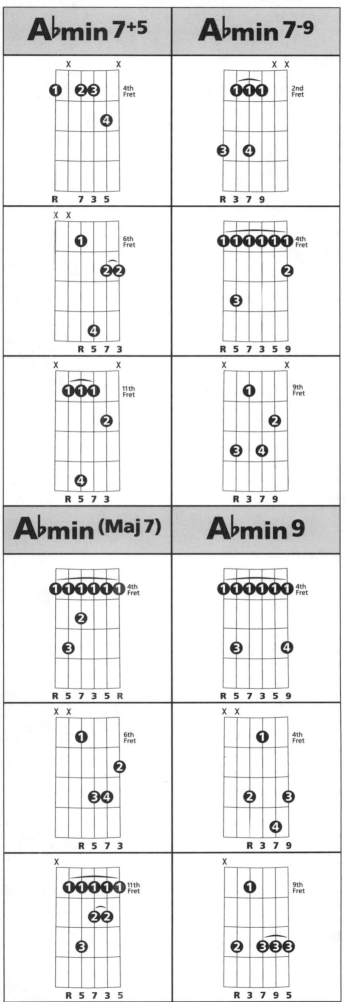

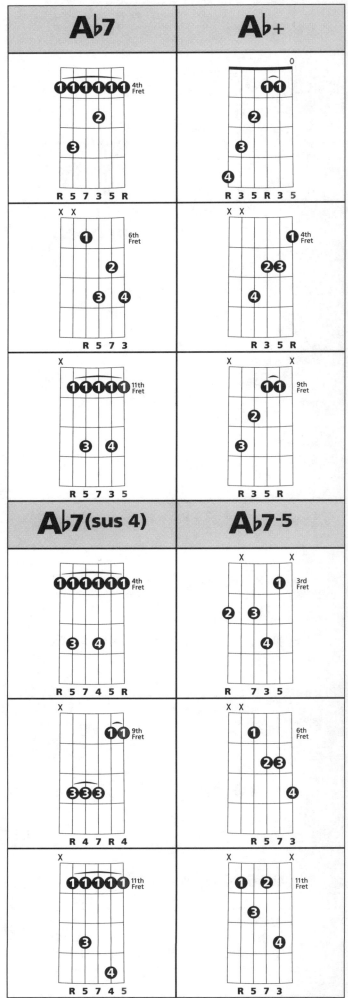

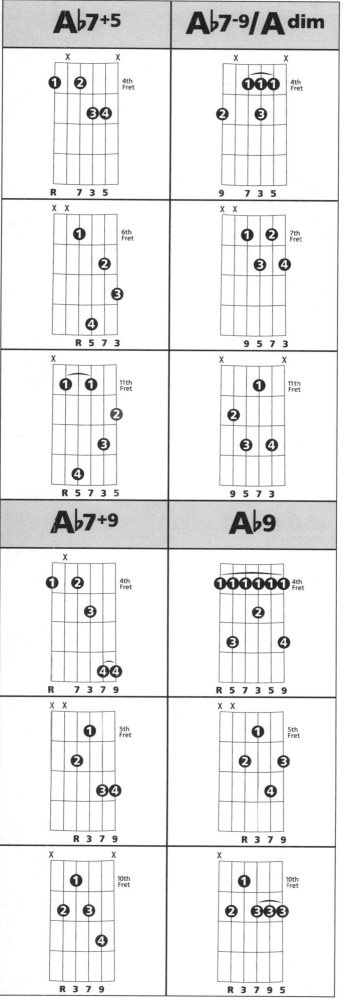

A♭9-5

R 3 7 9 5 R

R 5 7 9

R 3 7 9 5

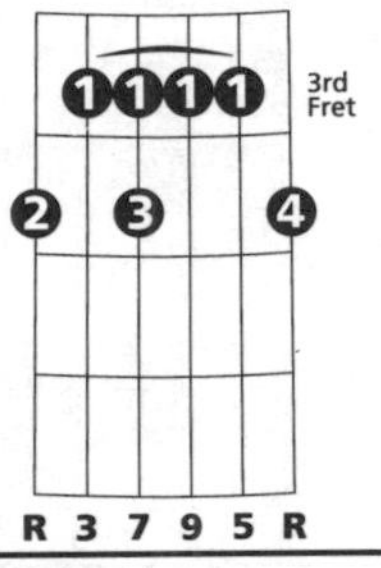

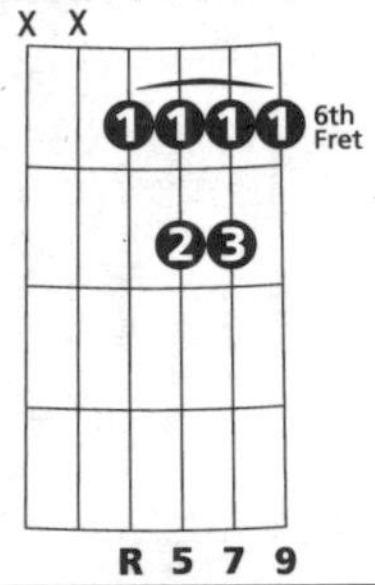

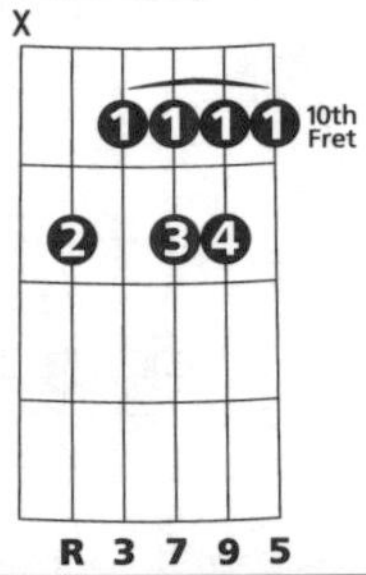

A♭9+5

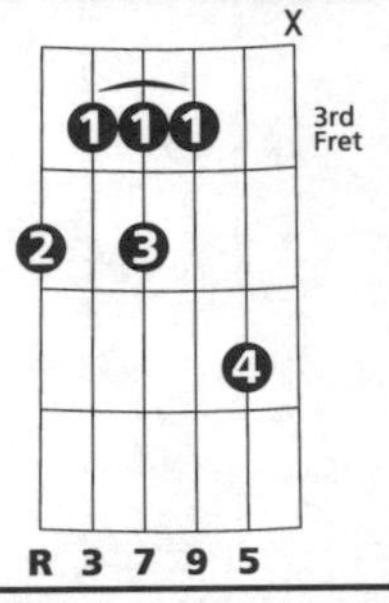

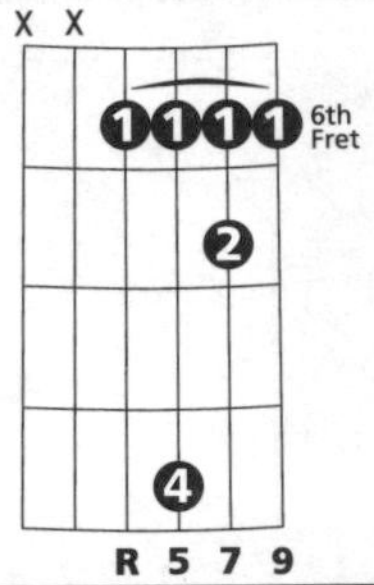

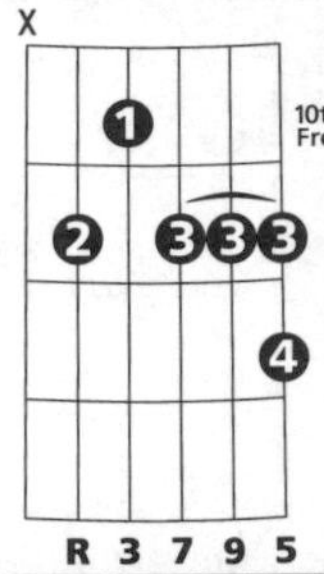

R 3 7 9 5

R 5 7 9

R 3 7 9 5

A♭11

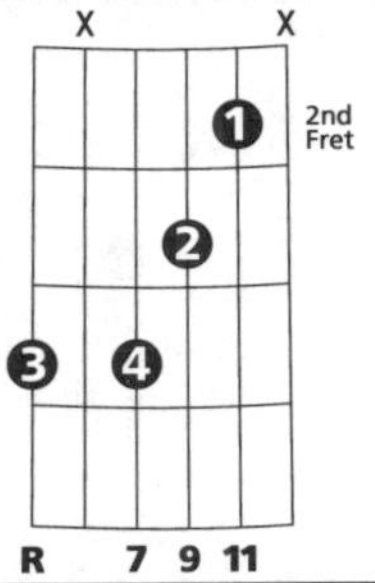

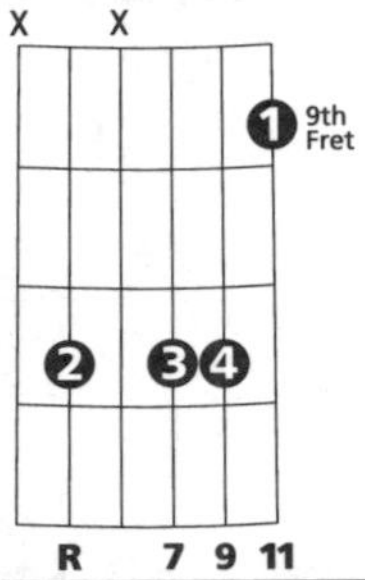

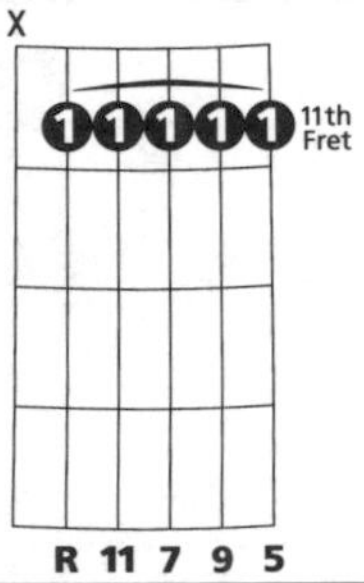

R 7 9 11

R 7 9 11

R 11 7 9 5

A♭13

R 7 9 3 13

R 7 3 13

R 3 7 9 13

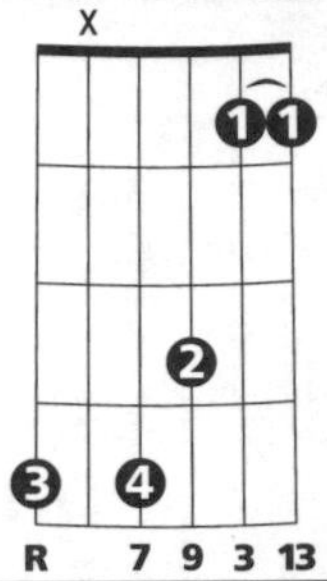

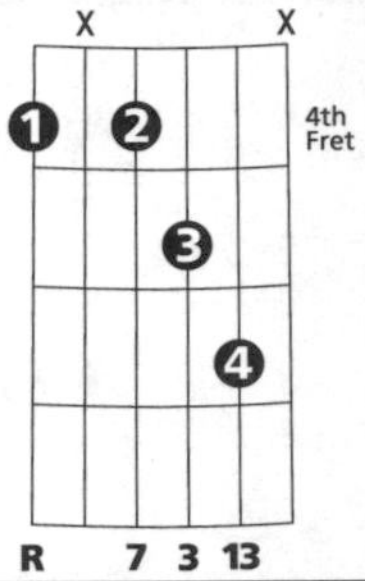

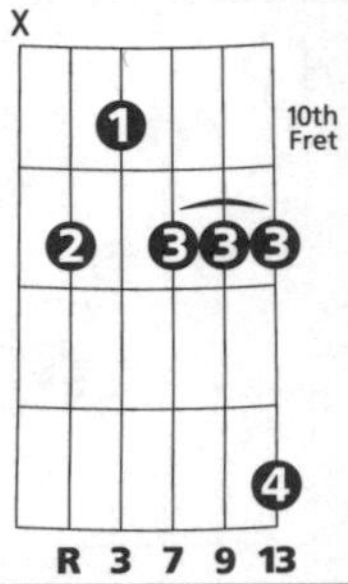

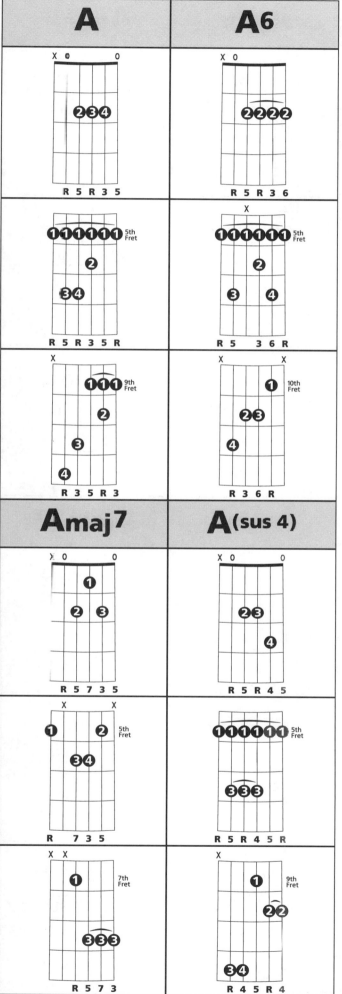

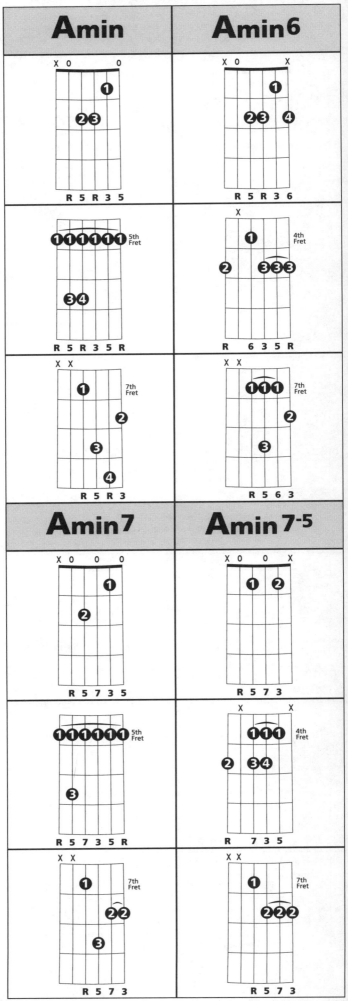

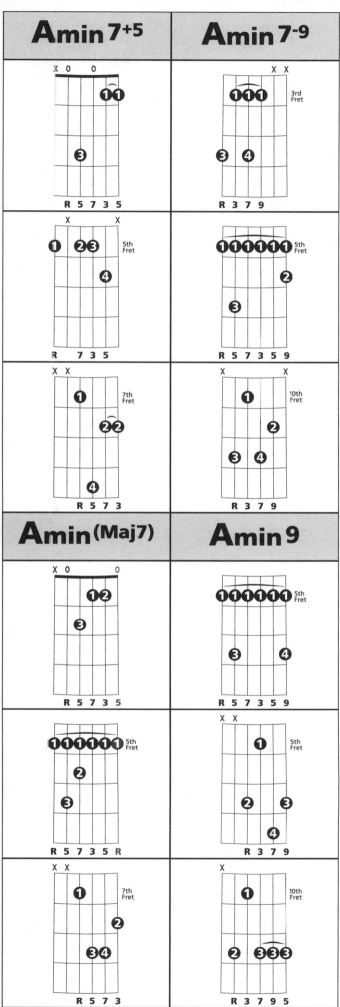

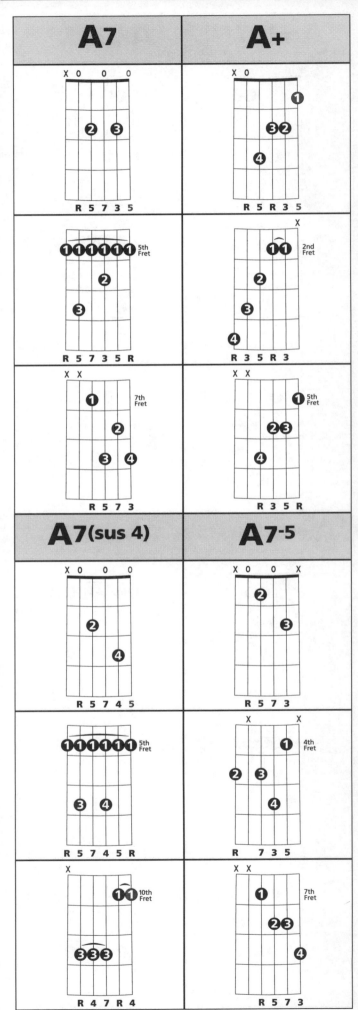

Root: A
Harmonic Function: Seventh

A7+5

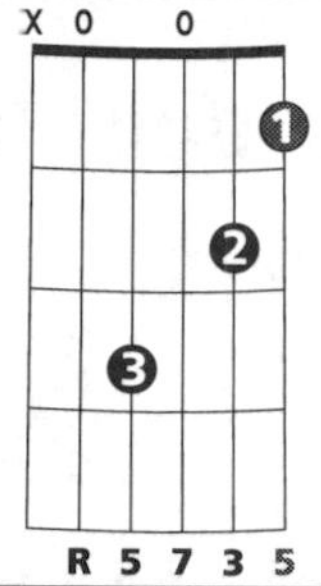

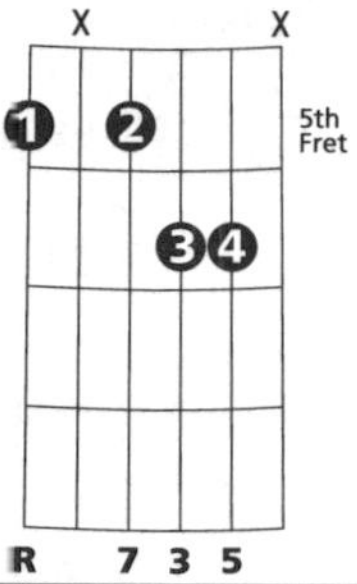

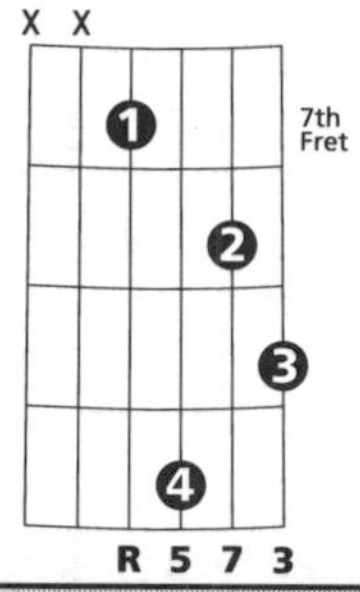

X O O
1
2
3
R 5 7 3 5

X X
1 2
3 4
5th Fret
R 7 3 5

X X
1
2
3
4
7th Fret
R 5 7 3

A7-9/B♭dim

X O X
1
2 3
9 5 7 3

X X
1 1 1
2 3
5th Fret
9 7 3 5

X X
1 2
3 4
8th Fret
9 5 7 3

A7+9

X
1 2
3
4 4
5th Fret
R 7 3 7 9

X X
1
2
3 4
6th Fret
R 3 7 9

X X
1
2 3
4
11th Fret
R 3 7 9

A9

1 1 1 1 1 1
2
3 4
5th Fret
R 5 7 3 5 9

X X
1
2 3
4
6th Fret
R 3 7 9

X
1
2 3 3 3
11th Fret
R 3 7 9 5

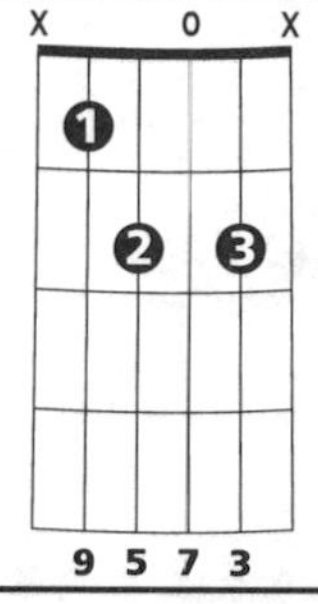

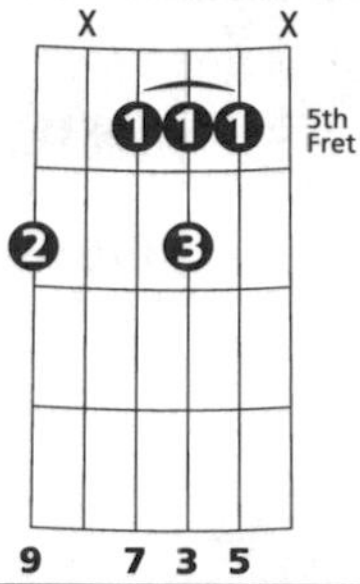

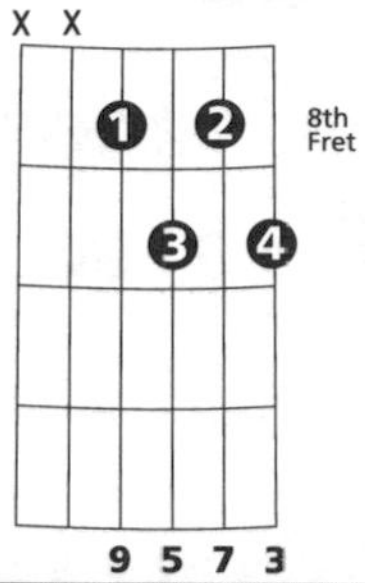

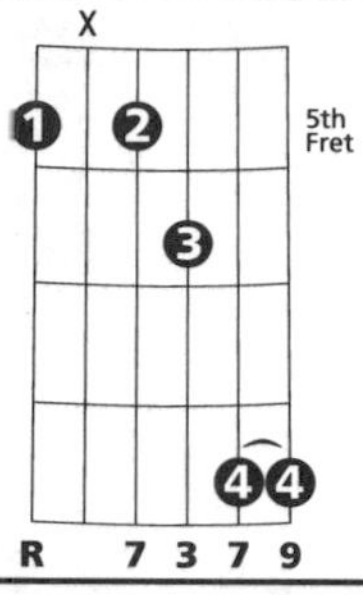

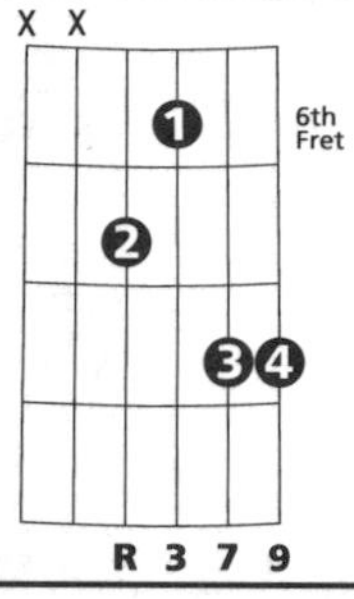

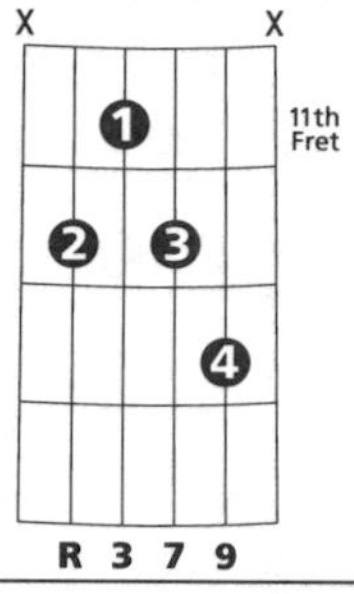

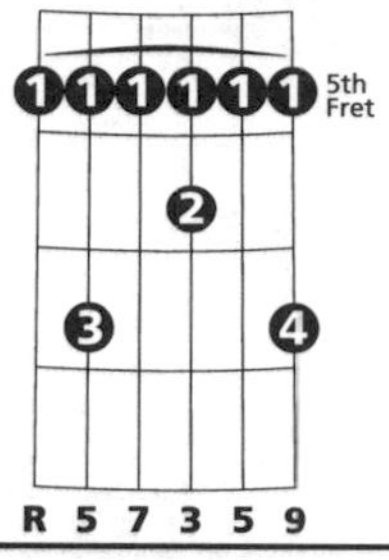

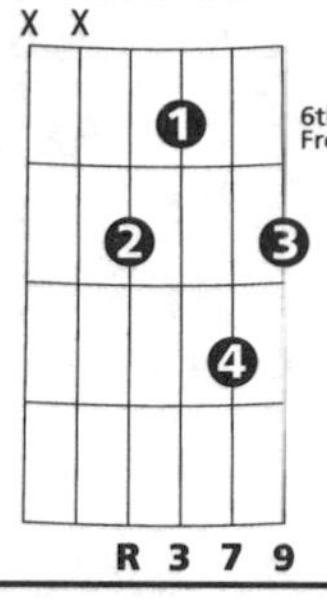

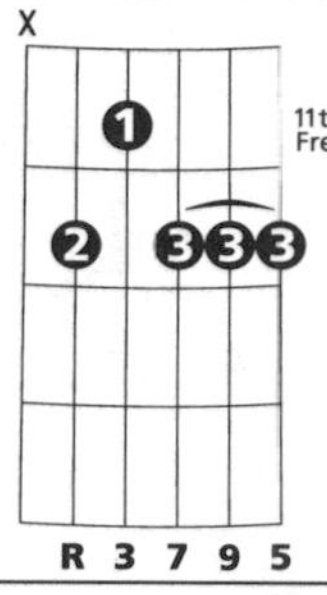

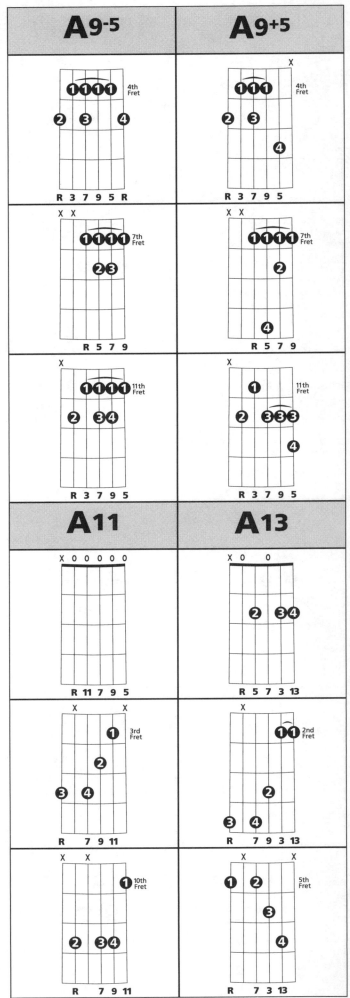

Root: B♭
Harmonic Function: Major

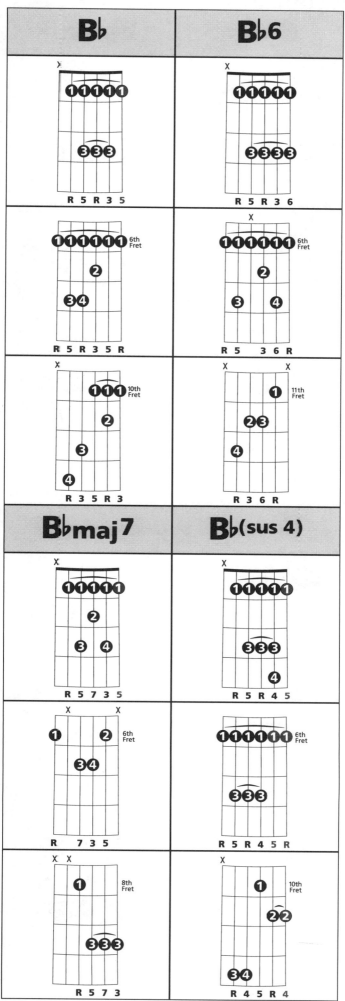

81

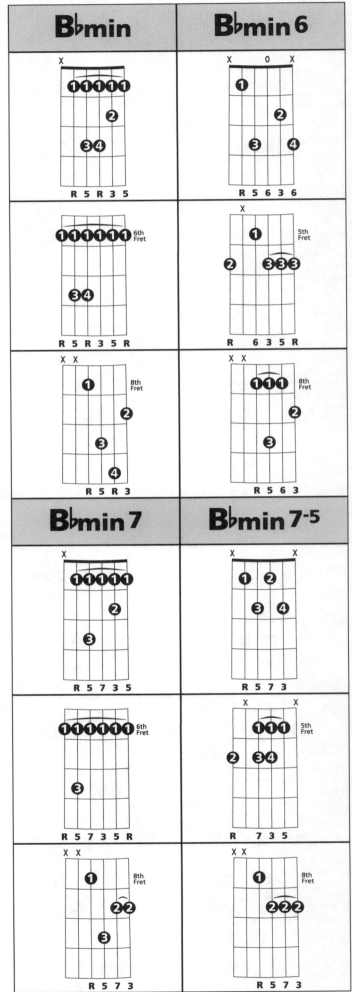

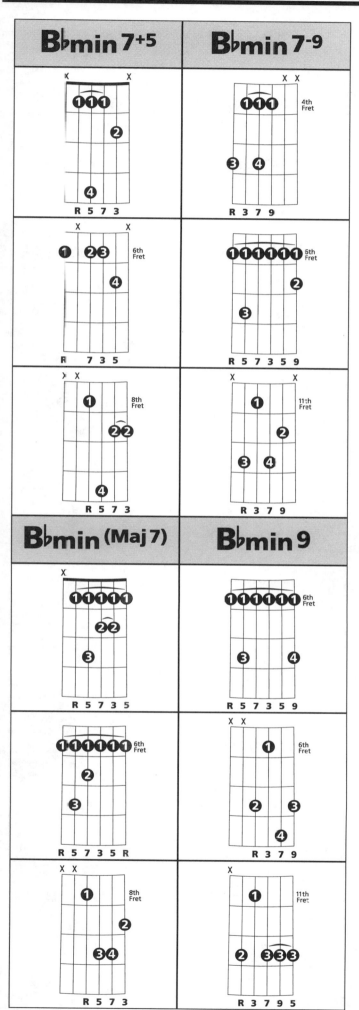

B♭min 7+5

B♭min 7-9

B♭min (Maj 7)

B♭min 9

Root: B♭
Harmonic Function: Seventh

B♭7

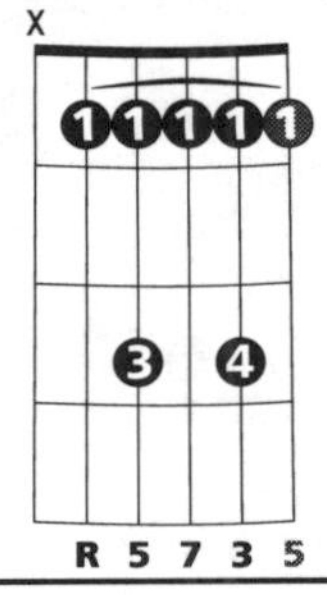
X
R 5 7 3 5

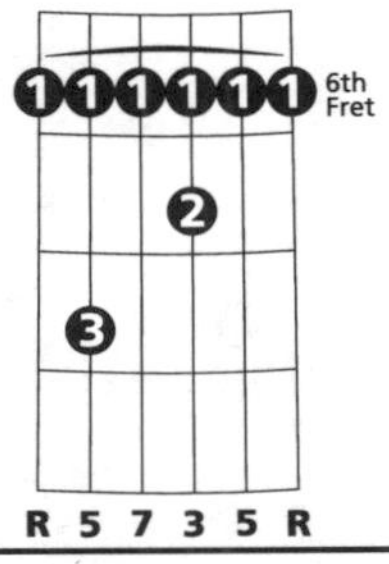
6th Fret
R 5 7 3 5 R

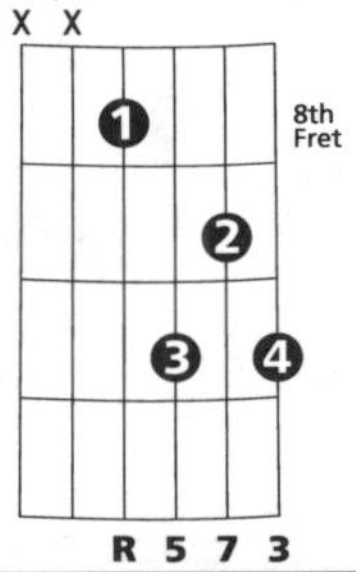
X X
8th Fret
R 5 7 3

B♭+

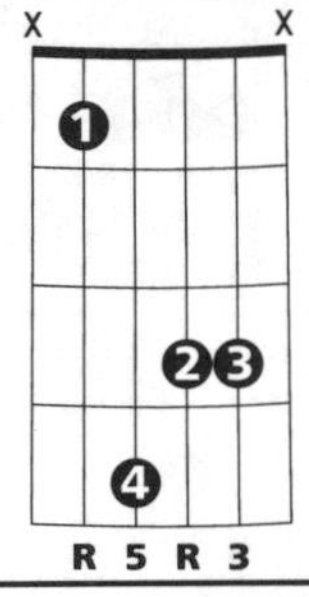
X X
R 5 R 3

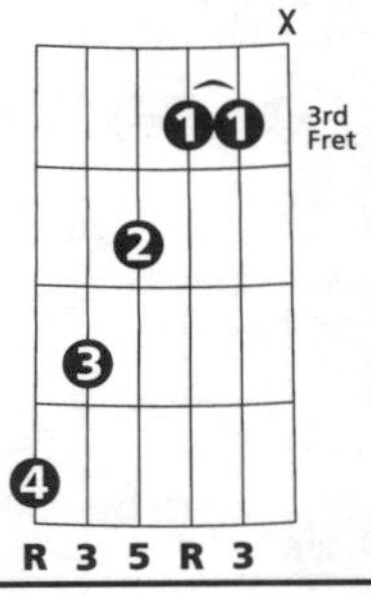
X
3rd Fret
R 3 5 R 3

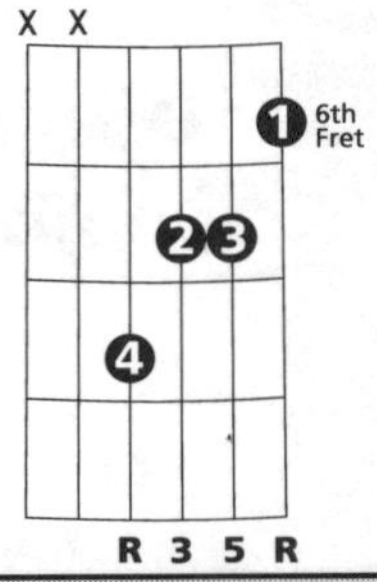
X X
6th Fret
R 3 5 R

B♭7(sus 4)

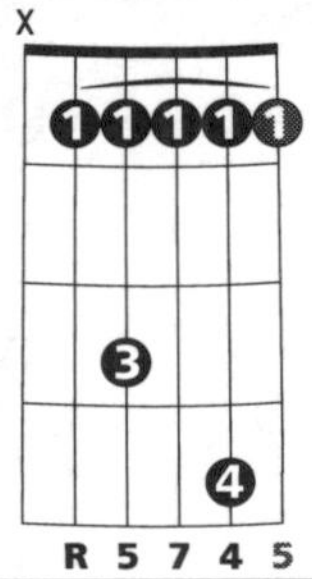
X
R 5 7 4 5

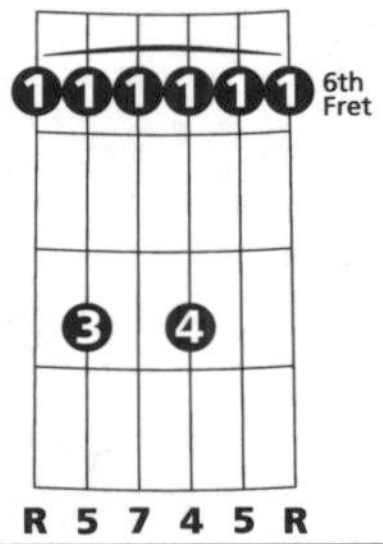
6th Fret
R 5 7 4 5 R

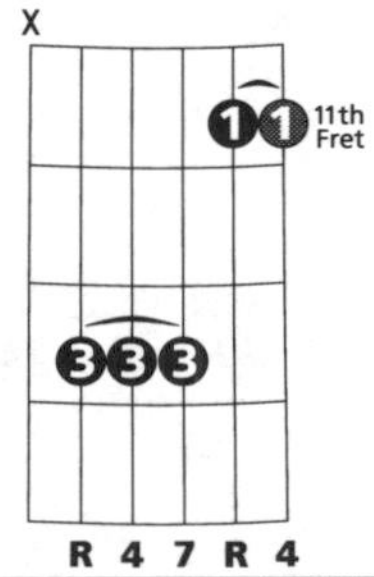
X
11th Fret
R 4 7 R 4

B♭7-5

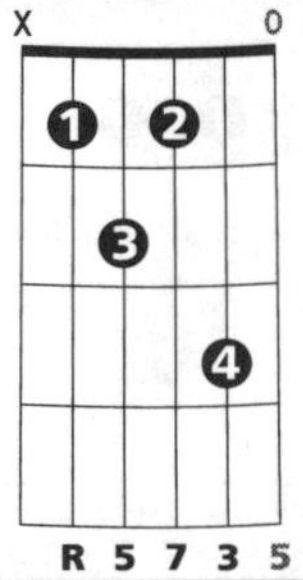
X 0
R 5 7 3 5

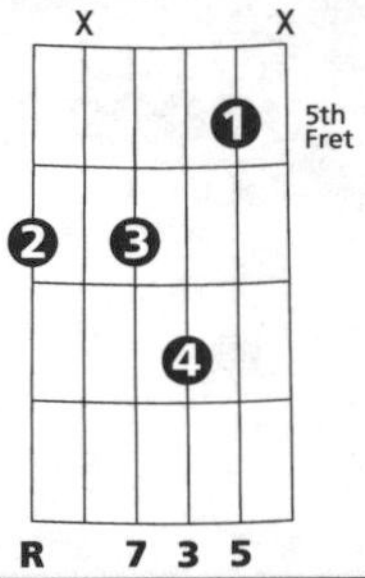
X X
5th Fret
R 7 3 5

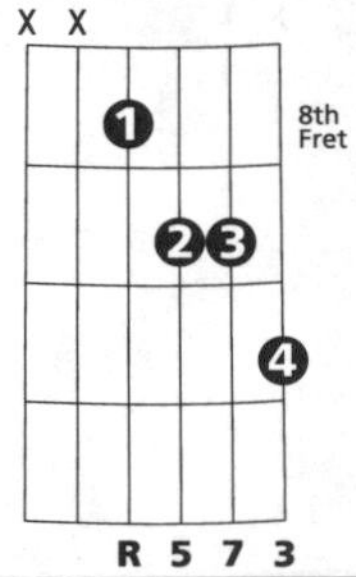
X X
8th Fret
R 5 7 3

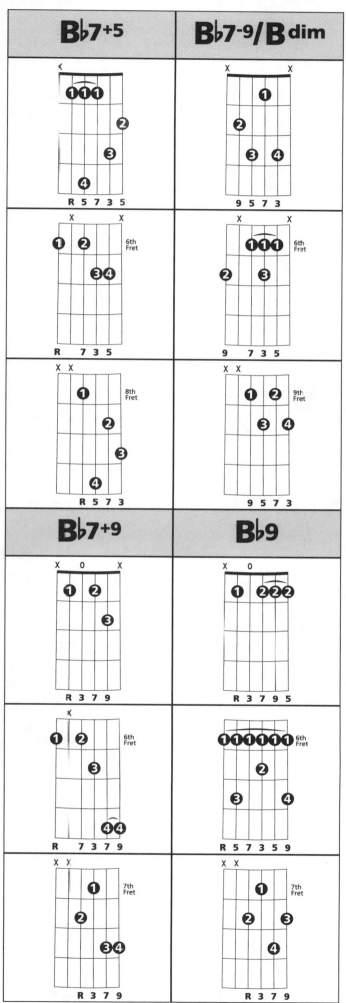

Root: B♭
Harmonic Function: Seventh

B♭9-5

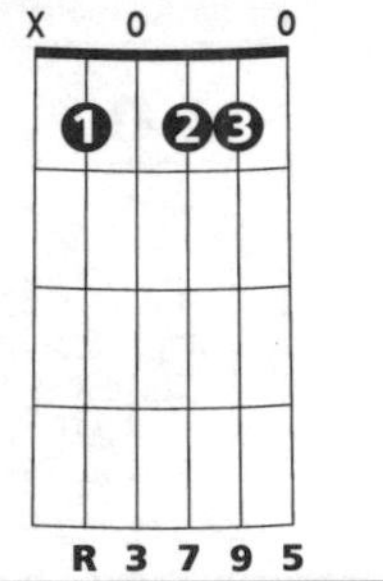
X 0 0
R 3 7 9 5

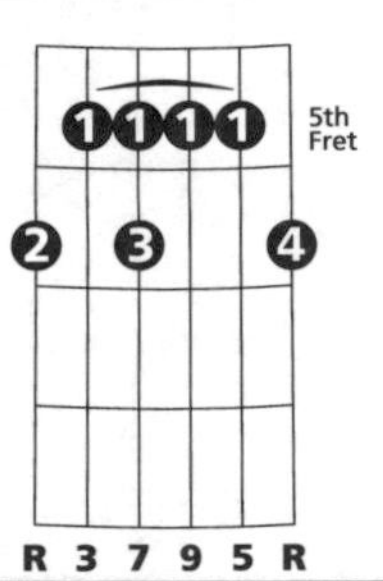
5th Fret
R 3 7 9 5 R

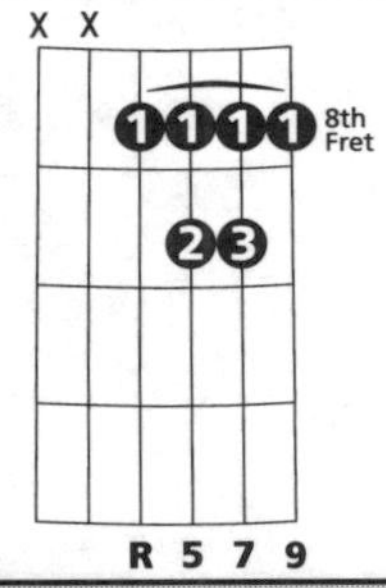
X X
8th Fret
R 5 7 9

B♭9+5

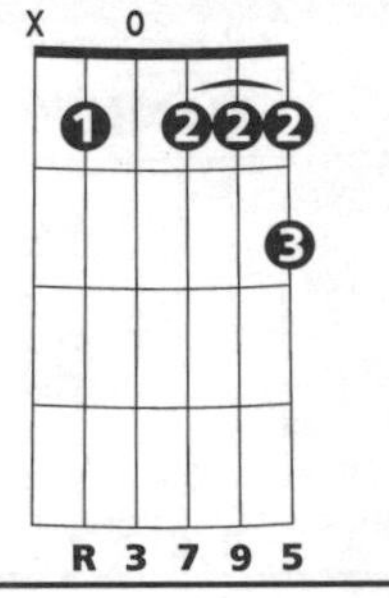
X 0
R 3 7 9 5

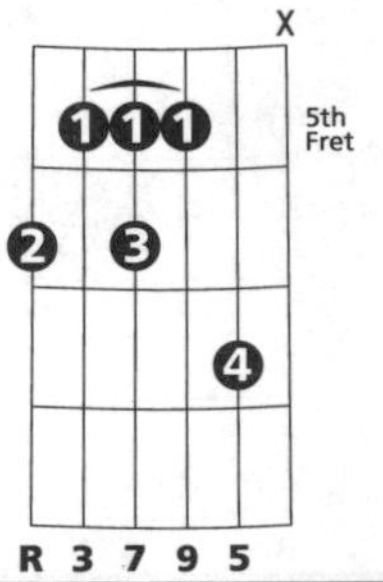
X
5th Fret
R 3 7 9 5

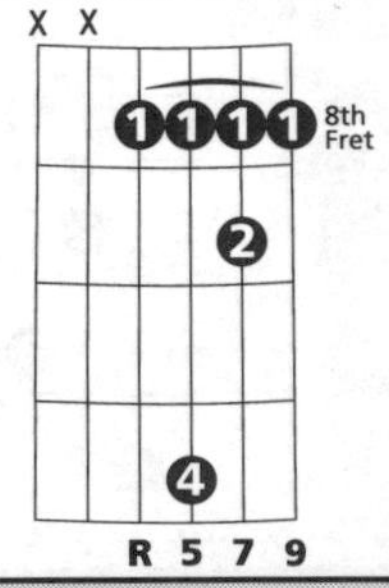
X X
8th Fret
R 5 7 9

B♭11

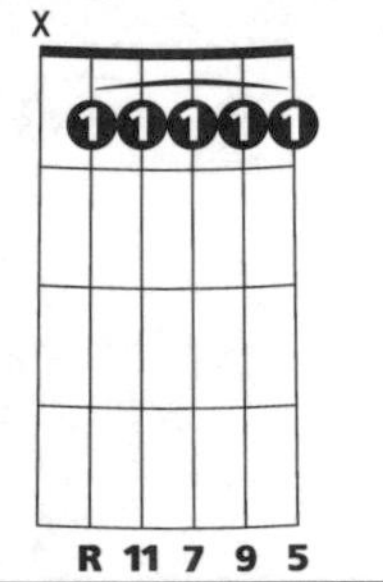
X
R 11 7 9 5

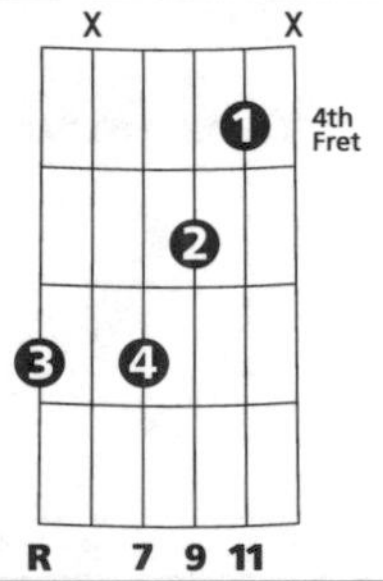
X X
4th Fret
R 7 9 11

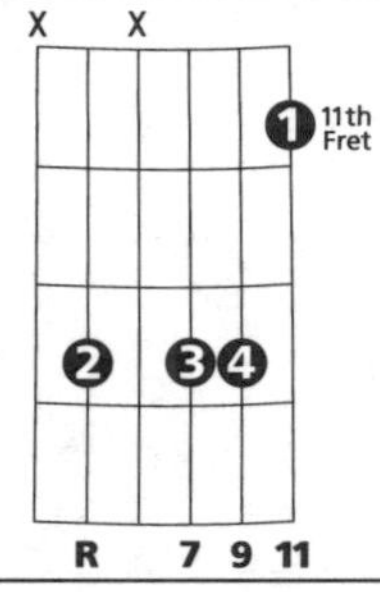
X X
11th Fret
R 7 9 11

B♭13

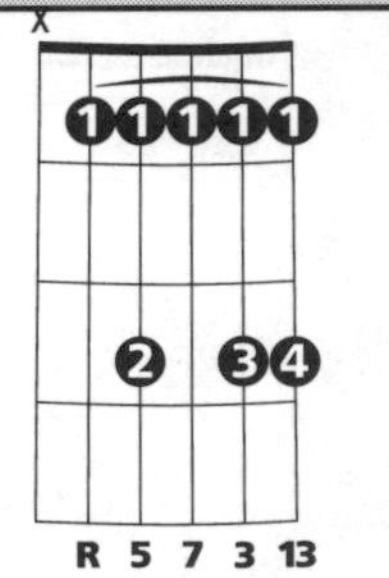
X
R 5 7 3 13

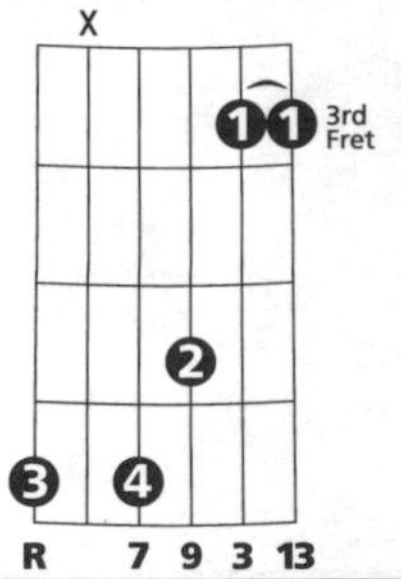
X
3rd Fret
R 7 9 3 13

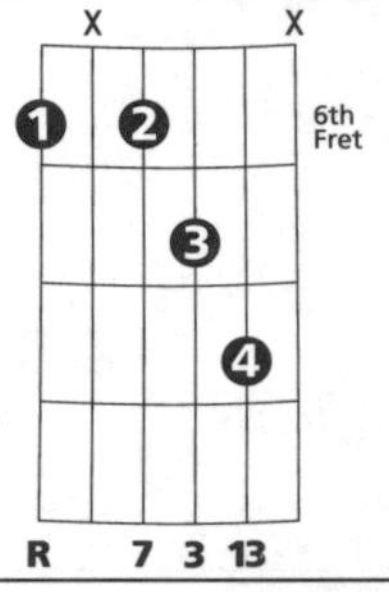
X X
6th Fret
R 7 3 13

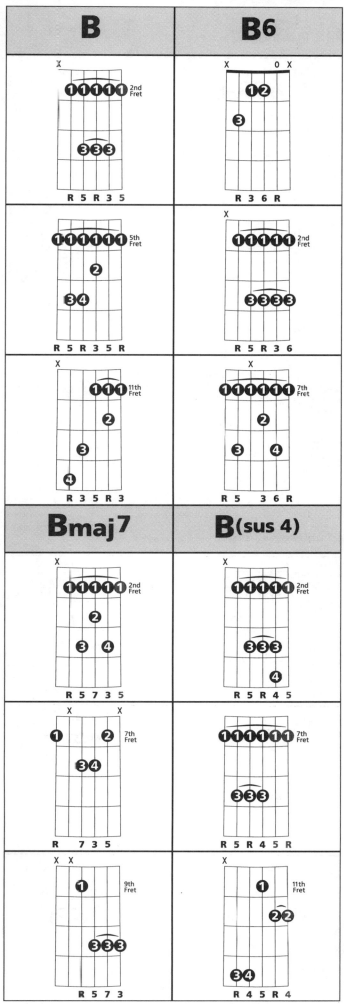

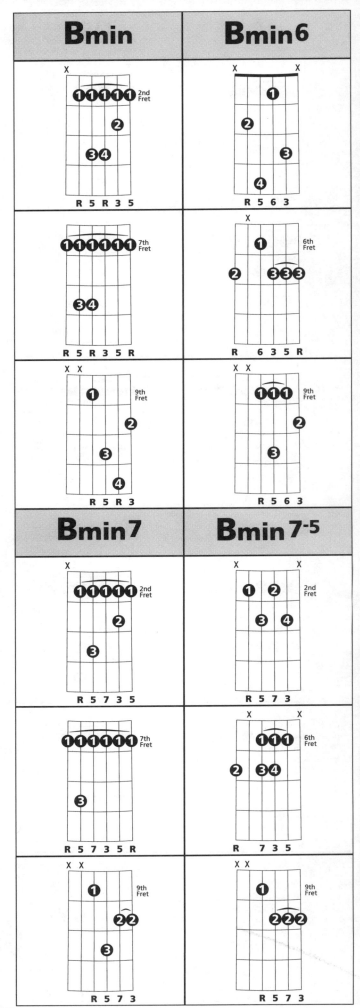

Root: B
Harmonic Function: Minor

Bmin	Bmin6

(Bmin, 2nd Fret: R 5 R 3 5)

(Bmin, 7th Fret: R 5 R 3 5 R)

(Bmin, 9th Fret: R 5 R 3)

(Bmin6, R 5 6 3)

(Bmin6, 6th Fret: R 6 3 5 R)

(Bmin6, 9th Fret: R 5 6 3)

Bmin7	Bmin7⁻⁵

(Bmin7, 2nd Fret: R 5 7 3 5)

(Bmin7, 7th Fret: R 5 7 3 5 R)

(Bmin7, 9th Fret: R 5 7 3)

(Bmin7⁻⁵, 2nd Fret: R 5 7 3)

(Bmin7⁻⁵, 6th Fret: R 7 3 5)

(Bmin7⁻⁵, 9th Fret: R 5 7 3)

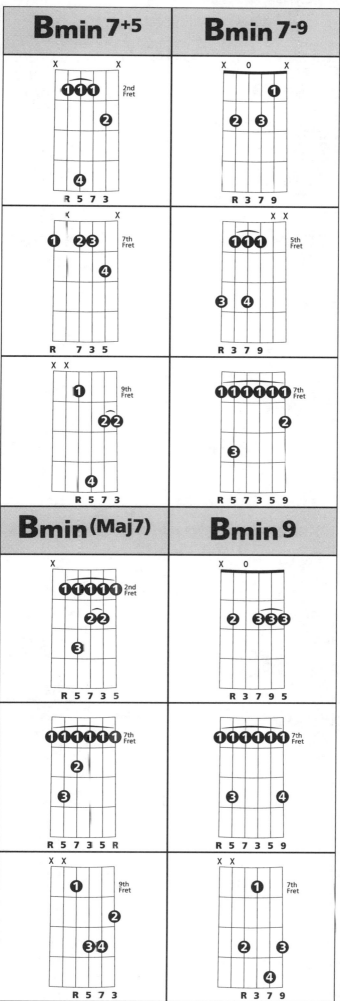

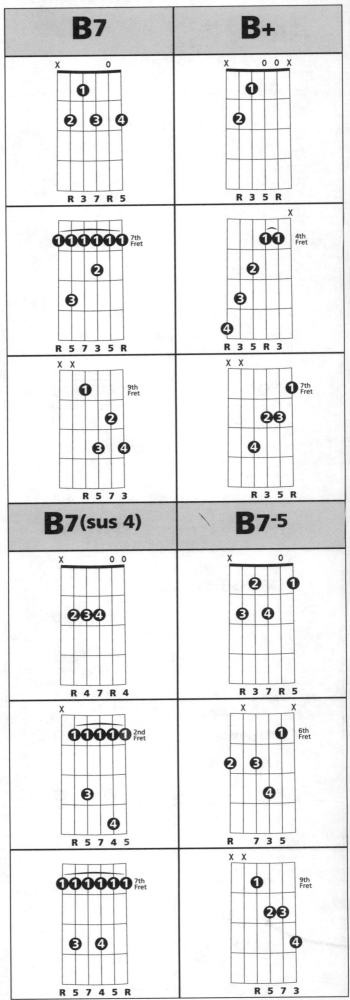

Root: B
Harmonic Function: Seventh

B7+5

X
0
R 3 7 R 5

X X
7th Fret
R 7 3 5

X X
9th Fret
R 5 7 3

B7-9/Cdim

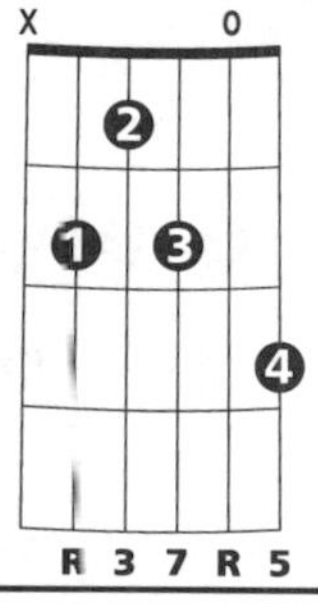

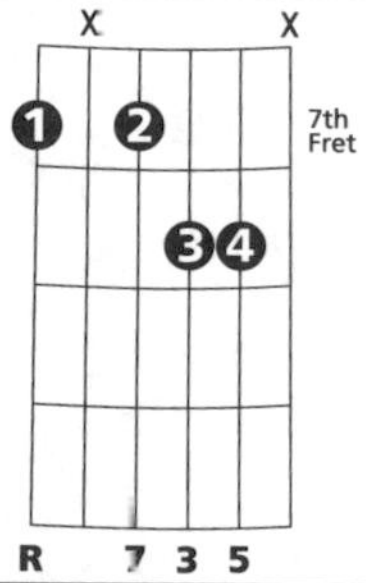

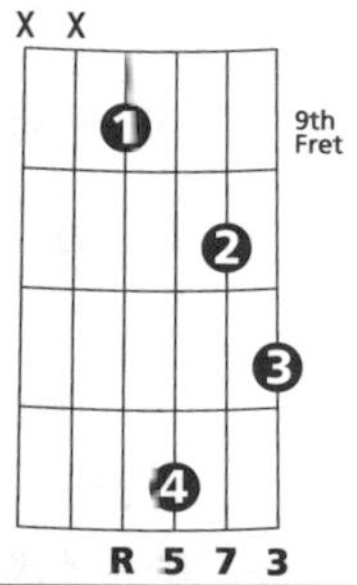

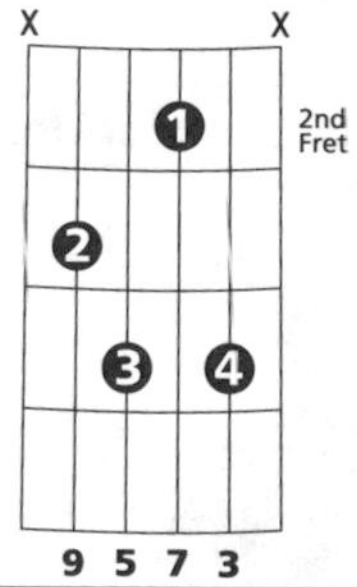

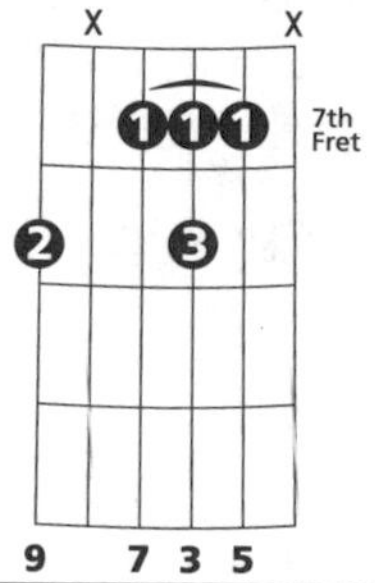

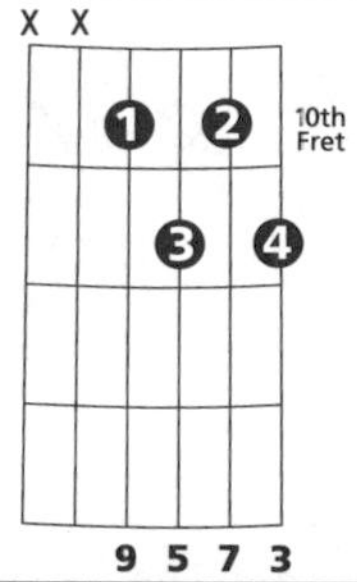

X X
2nd Fret
9 5 7 3

X X
7th Fret
9 7 3 5

X X
10th Fret
9 5 7 3

B7+9

X X
R 3 7 9

X
7th Fret
R 7 3 7 9

X X
8th Fret
R 3 7 9

B9

X
R 3 7 9 5

7th Fret
R 5 7 3 5 9

X X
8th Fret
R 3 7 9

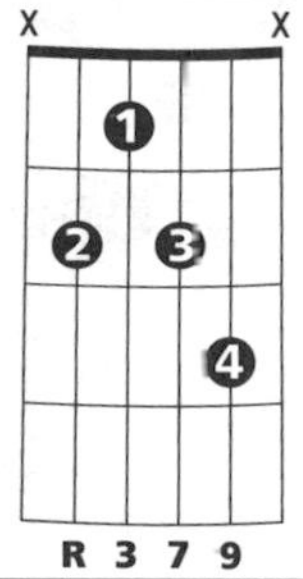

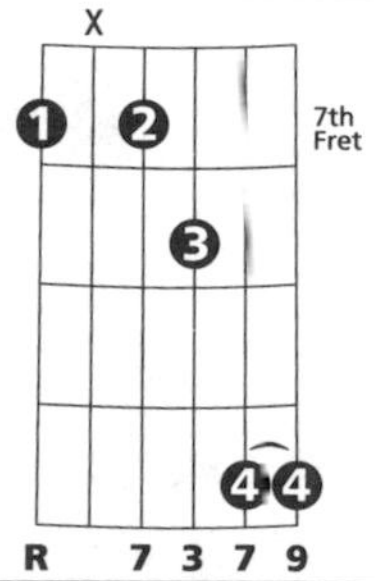

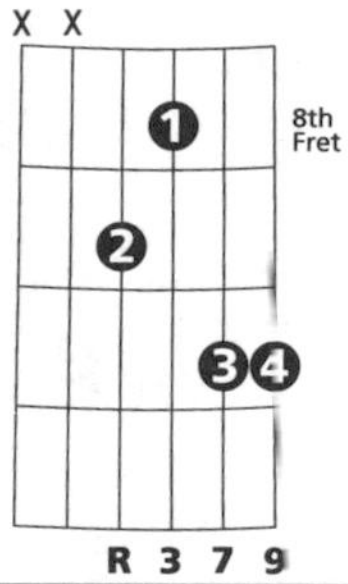

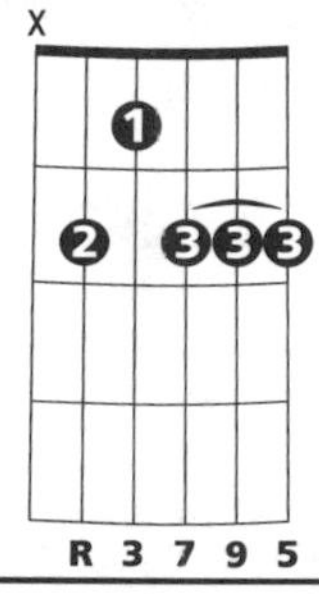

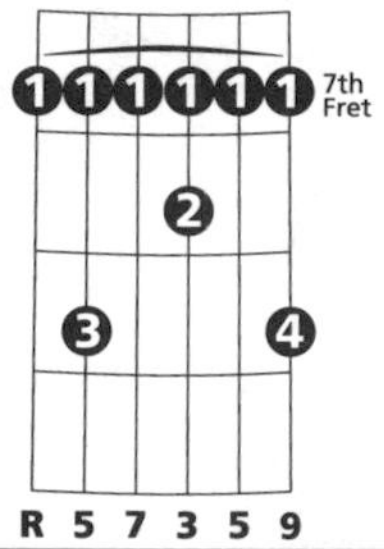

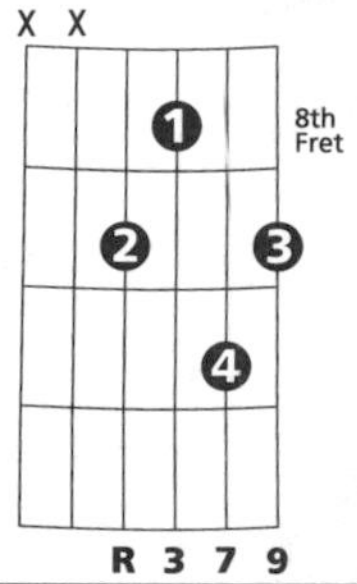

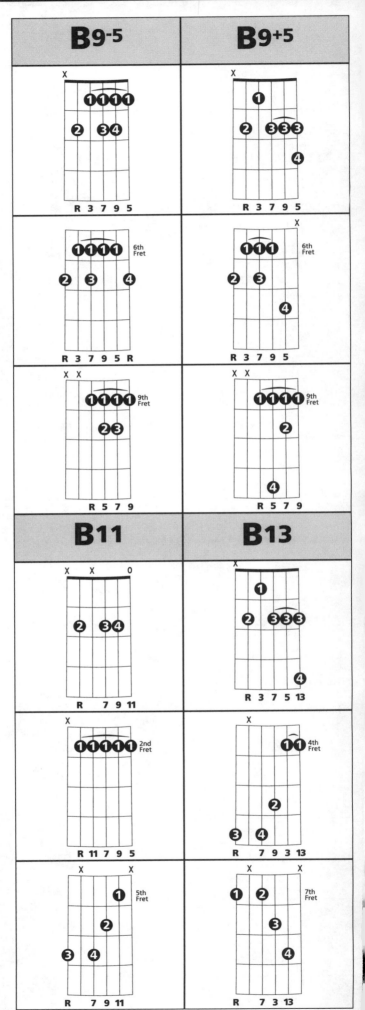

B9-5

B9+5

B11

B13

Psycho-acoustic Hierarchy

*T*here is a definite hierarchy or order of precedence that determines how the ear perceives music.
Notes, chords and inversions all play a role in this three level structure. In order of importance:

1. If nothing else is playing, the ear tends to hear a melody as being in a major or minor key. If a chord structure in the same tonality accompanies the melody, this reinforces the perception of the melody being in that key. For example a melody in C major accompanied by a C major chord will be clearly heard to be in C major. *(Example 1, below)*

2. If a different chord accompanies the melody, the melody will then appear to be in the key in which the new chord is the tonic.
    ### CHORDS RULE THE MELODY!
    For example, if our original melody in C major is now accompanied by an A minor chord, it will appear to be in the key of A minor. *(Example 2, below)*

3. If a bass note from another key is added to the accompaniment, the entire structure will now appear to be in the key in which the bass note is the tonic.
    ### BASS RULES THE CHORDS!
    In our ongoing example, if we add a G bass note to our melody in C accompanied by an A minor chord, the ear will perceive the whole structure to be in a G tonality of some kind. This is why chord inversions work differently than root position chords. *(Example 3, below)*

Modes

Modes, while derived from major scales, are harmonically quite distinct from them. The rules of substitution and alteration continue to apply, although chords will take different and distinct new harmonic functions in each mode. On these two pages, you will find diatonic triads (with one seventh chord) for each of the seven modes (Major is called the Ionian mode in the Greek modal system), along with the defining chord progressions (V7-I, or I-IV-V7, or ii-V7-I will define major). A defining progression is one which cannot exist in any other mode.

Each mode has its own unique sequence of half steps and whole steps which also helps identify it. For example, the half step between i & II in the Phrygian mode is as unique and important as the harmonic functions of the i & II chords themselves.

Ionian Mode (Major)

Scale degree	Type of Triad	Defining Progressions
I	Major	I - IV - V^7
ii	Minor	V^7 - I
iii	Minor	ii - V^7 - I
IV	Major	
V^7	Seventh	
vi	Minor	
viidim	Diminished	

Sequence of Half steps and Whole steps: whole - whole - half - whole - whole - whole - half

Dorian Mode

Scale degree	Type of Triad	Defining Progressions
i	Minor	i - ii
ii	Minor	i - IV^7
III	Major	
IV^7	Seventh	
v	Minor	
viidim	Diminished	
VII	Major	

Sequence of Half steps and Whole steps: whole - half - whole - whole - whole - half - whole

Phrygian Mode

Scale degree	Type of Triad	Defining Progressions
i	Minor	i - II
II	Major	
III^7	Seventh	
iv	Minor	
vdim	Diminished	
VI	Major	
vii	Minor	

Sequence of Half steps and Whole steps: half - whole - whole - whole - half - whole - whole

Modes

Lydian Mode

Scale degree	Type of Triad	Defining Progressions
I	Major	I - II^7
II^7	Seventh	
iii	Minor	
ivdim	Diminished	
V	Major	
vi	Minor	
vii	Minor	

Sequence of Half steps and Whole steps: whole - whole- whole - half - whole - whole - half

Mixolydian Mode

Scale degree	Type of Triad	Defining Progressions
I^7	Seventh	VII - I^7
ii	Minor	vi - VII - I^7
iiidim	Diminished	
IV	Major	
v	Minor	
vi	Minor	
VII	Major	

Sequence of Half steps and Whole steps: whole - whole - half - whole - whole- half - whole

Aeolian Mode (Natural Minor)

Scale degree	Type of Triad	Defining Progressions
i	Minor	i - iv - v
iidim	Diminishedr	VI - VII^7 - i
III	Major	
iv	Minor	
v	Minor	
VI	Major	
VII^7	Seventh	

Sequence of Half steps and Whole steps: whole - half - whole - whole - half - whole - whole

Locrian Mode

Scale degree	Type of Triad	Defining Progressions
idim	Diminished	idim
II	Major	
iii	Minor	
iv	Minor	
V	Major	
VI^7	Seventh	
vii	Minor	

Sequence of Half steps and Whole steps: half - whole - whole - half - whole - whole - whole

Blues, like any of the Greek modes is a different harmonic structure than major. Unlike modal or major constructions, however, all the chords in a Blues tonality are sevenths — that is, I^7, IV^7, V^7. That is the defining feature. All the standard seventh substitutions and alterations may be used, but the inherent dissonance of the seventh chords is never resolved.

Blues also differs from modal structures in that it is not built on, nor does it use the major scale or any of its modal derivatives.

Below is a table showing the notes in the blues scale (compared to a major scale), along with the way they may be interpreted in relation to each of the three pillar chords in a blues tonality structure.

As you can see each note of the scale can be interpreted as part of a standard substitute or altered chord. This is why you can play every note of a blues scale with every chord in a blues key (something that cannot be done in major or modal keys).

Scale Step (compared to Major)	In I7	In IV7	In V7
1	Root	5	sus4
♭3	♭3	♭7	+5
4	sus4	Root	♭7
♭5	♭5	♭3	+9
5	5	9	Root
♭7	♭7	4	♭3